HIP-HOP IN HOUSTON

HIP-HOP IN HOUSTON

the origin & the legacy

MACO L. FANIEL

FOREWORD BY STEVE FOURNIER & AFTERWORD BY JULIE GROB

Charleston   London

THE
History
PRESS

Published by The History Press
Charleston, SC 29403
www.historypress.net

Cover image courtesy of the Greater Houston Convention and Visitors Bureau (www.
visithoustontexas.com). Originally designed by GONZO247 of Aerosol Warfare Gallery/
Studio (www.aerosolwarfare.com).

First published 2013

Manufactured in the United States

ISBN 978.1.60949.978.5

Library of Congress CIP data applied for.

Notice: The information in this book is true and complete to the best of our knowledge. It is
offered without guarantee on the part of the author or The History Press. The author and
The History Press disclaim all liability in connection with the use of this book.

To Jordan Nimene-Mekhi Faniel

Broderick "50/50 Twin" Brown, Jukebox, K9/Sir-Rap-A-Lot

NC Trahan, Big Mello, Fat Pat, DJ Screw, Pimp C, Big Moe, Big Steve, A.C. Chill, Big Rue, Money Clip D, B.G. Gator, .38, Nut, Ray Barnett (Mourn Ya 'til I Join Ya)

CONTENTS

FOREWORD

For more than about twenty years now, I wondered if anyone knew of or even cared about how Houston, Texas, became one of the largest markets for hip-hop music in the world—and if anyone even knew the true history of how all this came to be. I always said that, one day, I would write a book to tell the story so that young rappers coming up could see what had happened for them to be able to enjoy the artistic freedom they have now—and also so that they would understand that if it weren't for Houston and the other southern states that followed, there would not have been the mass amounts of money made by the New York labels in the 1980s and '90s.

Well, thanks to Maco L. Faniel, I don't have to worry about that now, because the book you're about to read should answer any of the questions you might have about Houston's involvement in hip-hop and most of its hip-hop history. I have to give personal thanks to Maco for doing his research and talking to all the right people for this book, and also for telling a little bit of my story, which I've always been asked about over the years but never had the time to put down in writing. I think that after reading this book, you will find that Houston and its artists, producers, club DJs and early radio DJs affected the course of hip-hop music from its conception as it spread throughout the world. And now that the truth has been told, Houston can take its rightful place in the history of hip-hop as the most important influence outside of New York. Thank you, Maco L. Faniel.

STEVE M.J. FOURNIER

ACKNOWLEDGEMENTS

I approached the publication of this book with trepidation and reluctance because of the politics of my academic discipline/vocation. I spent a few weeks internally debating whether or not I would move forward with publishing this work. My answer came to me after an encounter with a longtime friend, Roderick "50/50 Twin" Brown.

I met Roderick in 1995 while playing basketball in the driveway of my boy Pistol's house. He and his twin brother (Broderick) were walking through the neighborhood trying to find something to do when they finally came upon our game of basketball. Everyone imagined that these two cats would not have any hooping skills, as they are both short, but they quickly surprised us. Over the next three years, we developed a friendship. We sometimes went to church together, we hooped together and we also began to try our hand at rapping. Our freestyle sessions took place at the house of my boy Pistol, who rigged up a way for us to record ourselves. My lyrical skills were subpar, but Roderick's and Broderick's were superb. By the end of high school, they were taking rapping more seriously, and I took going to college more seriously. As a result, they both began appearing on mixtapes for Swishahouse, Boss Hogg Outlawz and the Color Changin' Click. In 1999, Roderick was featured on the lead single "Big Ballin' Shot Callin'" for Swishahouse's debut album, *The Day Hell Broke Loose* (1999). Unfortunately, Broderick surrendered to the wiles of the streets, which led him to a forty-five year prison sentence for aggravated robbery with a deadly weapon and serious bodily injury. After his initial successes, Roderick was signed by Paid in Full Entertainment, where he recorded with Paul Wall, Chamillionaire and other members of the Color Changin' Click. Around 2004, Roderick created his own label, Roc 4 Roc Entertainment, where he continued to record albums. He is considered one of Houston's underground legends.

After high school, our interactions were sporadic, as we had chosen different paths. However, every few years, Roderick and I always seemed to find each other on Gulf Bank Street, the setting for many of our juvenile activities—good and bad. In the fall of 2012, we again found each other on Gulf Bank, as I was leaving my mother's house and he was chillin' in "the cut." Our conversation picked up where it had left off years prior— reminiscing and praising. I told him that I had dedicated my thesis to his brother Broderick and that I wanted to make sure that he received a copy. Fortunately, I had a copy in my car that I had been waiting to give him in the event that I ran into him. I gave it to him. Two days later, he called me excitedly, saying, "Bruh, you have to publish this because people need to know about this untold history." His words were calming; they spoke to the fears that I held about this project. His excitement and suggestion was a sign that this story is important for his identity and countless others whose agencies within hip-hop remain marginalized. Therefore, this narrative is not only a polemic but also an effort to tell the story of the early Houston hip-hoppers and their contribution to the culture. In the words of Jeezy, it is my attempt to "put on for my city!"

Now for the hard part—showing gratitude to those persons and or organizations who helped bring this project to fore. In hip-hop, this is called a "shout-out," because on a song or in the back matter of a CD, you get to mention the names of your homies and the places that are important to you and the project. Therefore, to keep it in the spirit of hip-hop, here are my shout-outs.

This text was possible only due to the firsthand knowledge of those still alive to describe how hip-hop in Houston developed and progressed during those early days. For this work, I conducted many interviews of persons who were agents in creating the culture. Without their stories, this investigation would have gone the way of other attempts to historicize Houston's hip-hop culture—a history that begins with the professionalization of the culture and that leaves out those persons and events that laid the groundwork. Therefore, it is with gratitude that I acknowledge the following persons for their assistance and their stories: Trena Foster, DJ Ready Red, Sire Jukebox, Def Jam Blaster, Luscious Ice, K-Rino, Ben Westoff, Raheem, Carlos Garza (DJ Styles), Lil' Troy, Willie D, Julie Grob, Thelton Polk (K9/Sir-Rap-A-Lot), Steve Fournier, Lester "Sir" Pace, Pam Collins, Wicked Cricket, Ricardo Royal, Jazzie Redd,

DJ Chill and Rashad Al-Amin. Three of these persons—Garza, Cricket and Al-Amin—were invaluable to my research, as they were able to connect so many dots and connect me with so many people. They are pioneers in their own right who are not often mentioned in the narrative because our understandings of hip-hop tend to only recognize those who perform or produce music or those who have reached a certain commercial status, yet these ambassadors represent for Houston in innumerable ways at home and on the road. To all the hip-hoppers from those early days, it is my hope that I've told your story accurately and that I've represented you well.

This work was also possible because of those who began and those who continued to write the hip-hop canon as a framework to understand American life and the various nuances of a generation and a people. The names include but are not limited to: Nelson George, Tricia Rose, Michael Eric Dyson, Joan Morgan, Raquel Cepeda, Murray Forman, Mark Anthony Neal, William Jelani Cobb, Pero Dagbovie, Brian Coleman, Dan Charnas, dream Hampton, Bakari Kitwana, Jeff Chang, Mickey Hess, Mtume Ya Salaam, David Mills, Derrick Aldridge, M.K. Asante, Yvonne Bynoe, Anthony Pinn, Brian Coleman, Jim Fricke, Charlie Ahearn, Steven Hager, Mickey Hess, Robin D.G. Kelley, Alex Ogg, David Upshal, William Eric Perkins, Imani Perry, Roni Sarig, David Toop, Kevin Powell, James Braxton Peterson, Jocelyn Wilson, Alan Light, Touré, Greg Tate, Marc Lamont Hill, Todd Boyd and Jeffery O.G. Ogbar. I look up to them all, and I thank them all for making hip-hop a viable subject matter. There are also trailblazers in the writing of Houston hip-hop that I am indebted to: Andrew Dansby, Matt Sonzala, John Nova Lomax, Lance Scott Walker, Chris Gray, Shea Serrano and many others.

During the brainstorming for this project, I thought it important to investigate Houston's black music traditions to determine if there were any connections to hip-hop in Houston and to argue that just as Houston hip-hop is largely disregarded, so are its other forms of popular black music. My questions about the black music traditions in Houston first led me to the work of Roger Wood, and I researched many of the names and places mentioned in his texts. In the process, I found myself falling in love with people and music that I never knew about. Every time that I found a new piece of information or a new connection, I became even more excited and proud of my city. While at a meeting at the African American Library at the Gregory School, I came across a board member, Lizette Cobb, whose last name sounded familiar. When I asked her if she was related to Arnett Cobb, she said, "Yes, he is my father." In reply, I said, "I need to talk to you about this project I am doing!" We then began talking periodically about Houston's jazz history. Lizette introduced me to the Texas Jazz Archive, which served as a valuable resource for this project. I am now a greater champion of Houston's music culture after finding out how deep and rich it is. Thank you to Roger, Lizette and Tim (from the Texas Room at the Houston Metropolitan Research Center).

While writing this book, I found it difficult to write at home. In my efficiency apartment, I felt closed in and lonely, and I often became distracted. Therefore, I spent a lot of time at coffee shops and other places that offered free Wi-Fi, where I was able to pick up on the energy of others attempting to be creative. These places include, the Doshi House, the Eat Gallery, Blacksmith Coffee Bar and Boomtown Coffee. I am also thankful for the staff at the African American Library at the Gregory School for helping me find texts needed for my research and for conversing with me during my many moments of distraction.

I would also like to thank my friends who encouraged me during the days that I wanted to give up and who also read over several iterations of this project: Cleve Tinsley, Camesha Scruggs, Arlisha Norwood, Michelle Smith, Aundrea Matthews, Shannan Johnson, Tilicia Johnson, Lanecia Rouse, Meshah Hawkins and Jason Miller. There are also those friends and mentors who long ago told me that I should write a book—they saw things in me that I did not see or that I was too afraid to do: Kenneth Cotton, Rudy Rasmus, Odin Clack, Christian Washington, Craig Bowie, Catheryn Longino, Nykeki Broussard, Pam Bryant and Terric Ayers.

I am tremendously grateful to my faculty mentors and my thesis committee, who all provided guidance, support, critiques and rebukes. Thank you, Finnie Coleman, Cary Wintz, Merline Pitre, Roger Wood, Daniel Adams and Nupur Chaudhuri for serving on my committee, adding to my life and pushing me to be a competent scholar. I owe special shout-outs to Dr. Coleman, Dr. Wintz and Dr. Chaudhuri. Dr. Coleman has been a mentor and friend for the last fifteen years and is one of the key figures in my decision to pursue the life of the mind. He was my first example of a black man from "da hood" in the academy, and he allowed me to imagine a vocation beyond the perfunctory expectations of my community. I was first introduced to hip-hop as an academic subject through his Introduction to Hip-Hop Culture class in 2001. He constantly pushes me to read, to write, to critique life, to be a scholar instead of a student and to be a standup guy. Dr. Wintz made me a historian, and Dr. Chaudhuri helped me fall in love with counter-historical narratives, particularly those that challenge imagined communities.

ACKNOWLEDGEMENTS

I would be remiss if I did not thank my mother and grandmother. My mother was my first teacher of context, particularly the context of music. I love music because it was constantly played in my house and in her car. I love to think about the message of music, because she asked me questions about her music or testified about it herself. She and my grandmother were constant champions of this endeavor. Though neither one of them knew what I was writing about, they kept asking me, "How is your book coming?" or "Are you finished with that book yet?" It has been my constant aim to make them proud. I hope they are proud of this.

To my editor, Christen Thompson, I thank you for encouraging me to go forward with this project, for your detailed editing, for overseeing this project and for your coolness.

To all of you who read this book, I hope that you enjoy it. Thank you for your support and for sharing this work with others. I hope that this book has broadened your understanding of history and also your knowledge of hip-hop.

Last but certainly not least, I am thankful to God, for in ways that I can't understand or explain, you orchestrated all of this, which amazes me and humbles me at the same time.

INTRODUCTION

Every generation has the opportunity to write its own history, and indeed it is obliged to do so. Only in that way can it provide its contemporaries with the materials vital to understanding the present and planning strategies for coping with the future. Only in that way can it fulfill its obligation to pass on to posterity the accumulated knowledge and wisdom of the past, which, after all, give substance and direction for the continuity of civilization.
—*John Hope Franklin, 1986*[1]

To begin, I believe that the question of how I came to this particular subject must be answered. I consider it a serendipitous matter—I was born at the right time, and I was on the Internet at the right time.

During the Christmas holiday of 2010, I found myself engaging in one of my oft-practiced forms of procrastination from reading or writing—Facebook. This adventure brought me to a post on a friend's page that immediately grabbed my attention, as it featured two of my favorite persons: Jay-Z and Cornel West. It was a link to a videoed chat with Jay-Z, Cornel West and Paul Holdengräber at the New York Public Library titled Decoded: Jay-Z in Conversation with Cornel West.[2] Before I clicked on the link, I thought, "Wow, a merger of the street and the academy—this should be interesting!" Then I watched, and I was far from disappointed.

In summary, the video featured a conversation among the three about Jay-Z's book *Decoded*; Holdengräber questioned, Jay-Z explicated and West interpreted. This exchange made for an interesting dialogue, likened to a

Horatio Alger story, that depicted how a generation of marginalized citizens strived to come to the American center—living the American Dream—through and with hip-hop.

Jay-Z held Holdengräber spellbound by the way he was able to explain his life and hip-hop culture. He reasoned that his experiences (and those of many of the hip-hop generation) and the life experiences of Holdengräber were similar because although they faced different realities, they shared the same existential questions. His most poignant claim was that hip-hop must be understood in the appropriate context, else it falls victim to misunderstandings and lies.

As I listened, I began to experience an "aha" moment—a series of thoughts and memories began to race through my head. I thought about my experiences in church as a young minister having to provide context of the biblical narrative through sermons and bible studies, conversations with my mother about context in movies or songs, my firsthand experiences with hip-hop culture and its music (especially hip-hop from Houston), my experiences in my Introduction to Hip-Hop Culture class (circa 2001) and the misunderstandings of hip-hop culture. I then thought about the broader implications of Jay-Z's conversation about context. What other stories needed to be told to understand the context of hip-hop culture? What about the other figures and cities that helped to shape the hip-hop narrative? Then my racing thoughts finally slowed to a singular pace, and a clear thought emerged: "I want to study the historical context of Houston's hip-hop culture." A few weeks later, I submitted a proposal to my graduate advisor to make this subject the focus of my master's thesis. This text is an adaptation of that work.

Yet I don't know if this moment of clarity, which led me to decide on this subject, would have been possible if I were not born at the right time. Because hip-hop has always been a part of my world, as I have lived through each of the overlapping eras of hip-hop.[3]

I was born in Houston, Texas, in August 1980 at Jefferson Davis Hospital (the county hospital) to a nineteen-year-old unwed mother from the Fifth Ward community. My birth occurred twelve years after the assassination of Dr. Martin Luther King Jr., a date that some consider the end of the modern civil rights movement. This was a few months before the election of Ronald Reagan to the presidency of the United States of America. It was also less than a year after the release of "Rapper's Delight" and a year before the debut of MTV. My birth year fell during a time of considerable economic and residential growth for Houston. However, in contrast, ghetto communities like the Fifth Ward were not the lucky beneficiaries of this growth—only more crime, unemployment, education disparities and widespread nihilism. We lived in the Fifth Ward for the first four to five years of my life while my mother sorted out what she would do for vocation. After she began working as a postal carrier, we moved to the deep north side of Houston in the Greenspoint community, where we resided for the next eight years.

Although I have never lived in a world without hip-hop, its sounds did not dominate my elementary years. During those years, I grew to love the music that played on my mother's car radio and home stereo: funk, soul, "down-home blues" and R&B. Her songs were special to me because they were special to her. Unknowingly, she taught me much about life through her music selections. She was my first teacher of context because of her constant beckoning to make sure that I understood the meanings of certain songs. Three songs hold special significance: the Temptations' "Treat Her Like A Lady," Bobby Womack's "Woman's Gotta Have It" and the Commodores' "Zoom." She used the first two songs to teach me how to love a woman, because she wanted to make sure that I did better at it than the men that had failed her. The last song was her way of teaching me how to hope beyond momentary despair.

Even though hip-hop began to make noise in the '80s, it was still in its nascent years, too young for my mother, a young adult in Houston. I can't say that she hated hip-hop; she just never caught on to the culture. Therefore, I only heard hip-hop when hanging with cousins or intermittently on local black radio stations or MTV.

This all changed between 1988 and 1992. For a brief period, I had an older stepsister and stepbrother that both had access to rap music. On television, I was able to see hip-hop more because of *Yo! MTV Raps* and the *Arsenio Hall Show*. I also received my first stereo and Walkman, which gave me control over the music that I listened to. At ten, I received my first rap tape, MC Hammer's *Please Hammer, Don't Hurt 'Em*. I learned the lyrics to the Geto Boys' classic song "Mind Playing Tricks On Me," which hit the airwaves in 1991. In that same year, 97.9 The Boxx (KBXX) launched in Houston as a radio station devoted to hip-hop and R&B music. In 1992, I went to my first rap concert to see Kriss Kross perform. At the end of 1991, my mother began a three-year separation that eventually resulted in a divorce. As a result, she had less time and energy to pay attention to my daily activities, and I had more time to develop my own tastes in music, listen to music that she did not necessarily approve of and get into adolescent troubles.

INTRODUCTION

My mother's divorce took us from Greenspoint to Acreage Homes (Acres Homes, Da 44) during the early years of the Modern Era of hip-hop (1992–1997). In the summer of 1994, my friend Pistol (Craig Joe) introduced me to a distinct music form that had emerged out of the south side of Houston two to three years earlier. This music form was known as "screwed" or "chopped and screwed." The creator of the form, DJ Screw (Robert Earl Davis Jr.) not only employed classic hip-hop DJ techniques such as mixing, scratching and backspinning but also made his style distinctive by slowing the tempo and reducing the pitch, giving the song a mellower sound and an increased focus on the lyrics. These mixtapes, known as Screw Tapes, were made on grey Maxwell cassettes that Screw sold out of his home. Screw featured popular songs on his mixtapes and also included freestyle raps from friends and neighborhood rappers. This phenomenon quickly spread throughout Houston and to cities and towns throughout Texas and Louisiana.

My friends and I listened to Screw tapes fervently for about two years. To our Screw tapes, we added chopped and screwed mixes that were created by DJ Michael "5000" Watts from the north side of town. Like the young people who began to mimic what they heard from the hip-hop mixtapes that traveled through New York in the late 1970s and after "Rapper's Delight," we began to freestyle and make our own tapes to be greater participants in the culture. These were the budding days of a genre within hip-hop that would take the world by storm a few years later.

Though my life was consumed by the Screw phenomenon, I was also inundated with various local, regional and national sounds that made my high school years a wonderful experience. These sounds included: UGK, Tupac, Biggie, Snoop Dogg, Bone Thugs N' Harmony, Puff Daddy, Crucial Conflict, Tela, Master P and No Limit, New Orleans Bounce and much more. Hip-hop music, in its various forms during that time, spoke to and of my personal experiences or spoke of things that I wanted to experience to earn masculine or ghetto stripes. At times, it was a surrogate father, teaching me lessons about life and women. I had spiral notebooks full of hip-hop lyrics that my friends and I transcribed; I partied to it, hooped to it, cleaned the house to it, washed my car to it, burst speakers playing it too loud and tried to write it and perform it.

In the summer of 1998, I entered my freshman year at Texas A&M University, and though I considered myself a fan and participator in the culture, I had a very limited hip-hop music collection. I met friends from all over the nation who were able to quote Wu Tang, Nas, Jay-Z and various other artists' music verbatim. I knew only the radio stuff, as my music collection was full of Screw tapes, Michael Watts mixtapes and other local and regional music. Although hip-hop was now mainstream, I did not have a need to listen to hip-hop music outside of my city/region because there was so much rich music that came out of Houston and because at that time, the local radio station supported local music.

Later, in my undergraduate career, I took a groundbreaking class taught by Finnie Coleman. This course, Introduction to Hip-Hop Culture, was groundbreaking because it was held at a traditionally conservative institution and because hip-hop studies was still a new academic field. It was in this course that I really learned how to read (paradigmatically instead of word for word), learned how to look at life critically and learned how to analyze hip-hop as a culture and as literature. This class seemed like my life on display—my life as an African American male living at the last twenty years of the twentieth century—investigated through a hip-hop literary framework.

On the first day of class, Dr. Coleman announced that we would be learning about life and death. I thought that he was crazy in saying that, because all I wanted was an A, but as I matured through adulthood, I came to understand him. Critical analysis of this culture meant a look at the ways in which a generation of young people in particular spaces and places struggled to live the American Dream and how they expressed themselves in the process. Never did I think that I would want to do more research about this subject, but I was called to it as a form of social justice.

This work, then, is important to me because I believe that hip-hop is an excellent discursive space to understand America, particularly the America lived in by those at the margins of society in the last quarter of the twentieth century. As such, a local history of hip-hop can offer an understanding of a city beyond beatific images and glorious stories. Further historical accounts through the framework of hip-hop culture are still limited. Thus, much of the understanding of African American life in America is based on a historical account that ends with the modern civil rights movement. This depiction and understanding discounts the life experiences of African Americans after this time period and also makes that time period the standard of African American life. To these points, to understand the life experiences of those African Americans born in a post Civil Rights–era Houston, whose cultural experiences were expressed through hip-hop, we cannot rely on narratives that exclude them or limit their contributions. Their hip-hop story must be told through their own contexts. Only then does a true continuum of knowledge exist between the generations.

Let me explain further.

There are various labels used to define the American experience for those African Americans born at the height of the civil rights movement and within twenty years of its end. The labels used often define this particular generation, born between 1965–1984, in relationship to their descendants—variously assigning them as beneficiaries, bastards, consumers or prodigals of their descendants. Robin D.G. Kelley noted that scholars and media sources have called this generation "a lot of things: the post soul generation, the post-civil rights generation, the postindustrial generation," "soul babies," and the "post-segregation" generation.[4] But journalist and activist Bakari Kitwana rescued this generation from limited definitions in opting for the "hip-hop generation" as an appropriate label.[5] Pero Dagbovie, a social and cultural historian specializing in hip-hop historiography, commented on Kitwana's conceptualization of the hip-hop generation by saying:

> *Shaped by the rise of multinational corporatism, globalization, neo-segregation, racialist public policy, the expanding media, and an overall poor quality of life for black youth, members of the hip-hop generation are linked mainly by the fact that we were born after the major struggles of the Civil Rights Movement and have collectively inherited a great deal from the battles waged by our elders. Echoing others, Kitwana noted that the hip-hop generation seems cut off from the social activist tradition associated with the Civil Rights-Black Power era.*[6]

This generation, the progenitors of hip-hop culture, "took the remnants of a dying society and created" a new narrative for the African American experience.[7] Hence, historical analysis of hip-hop culture is essential to understanding the ways in which this generation expressed and reflected its social, economic, political and personal realities through and with hip-hop. "Nonetheless," as Dagbovie claimed, "African American historians have not played a leading role in analyzing hip-hop or critically tapping into hip-hop culture as a viable discursive space for the black historical experience."[8] Yet history has much to offer to the study of hip-hop culture because history not only determines the origin and nature of a thing but also comments on the present and offers a guide for the future.

But we cannot dialogue or even historicize hip-hop culture without including regional and local sites, as the persons and practices within these sites were and are participators and creators in what we call hip-hop culture. Regional and local hip-hop cultural developments were not just modulations of East Coast and West Coast hip-hop; the culture progressed from local and regional domains. Thus, the history must be understood as a fragmentary development in which sedimentary parts come together to represent the nature of hip-hop culture.

If the Bronx represents that space and place of hip-hop's initial public offering, then the localities and regions that appropriated the culture increased its stock value. It is widely accepted that hip-hop culture became public as a result of the communal practices of young blacks and Latinos in New York boroughs and through the subsequent commodification of these practices by eager entrepreneurs. As hip-hop traveled out of the New York boroughs, young people—particularly African Americans and Latinos from the urban underclass—in other places began to negotiate their ghetto realities using hip-hop as their form of expression. Therefore, what we know as hip-hop culture is a special amalgamation of local and regional hip-hop particularities gone national and international— ultimately ghettoizing the world.

Historian William Jelani Cobb aptly framed the importance of space and place in hip-hop culture in his text *To the Break of Dawn: A Freestyle on the Hip Hop Aesthetic*, in which he differentiated hip-hop from previous genres/music cultures in writing, "While blues obsesses over the theme of mobility, hip-hop is as local as a zip code."[9] He continued:

> *In hip-hop…there are not references to highways or trains; railroads have been replaced by another central reference: the city. Or, more specifically, the fractured territories known collectively as the Ghetto. Innumerable hip-hop songs reference the term* [and] *all allude to a socio-economic blind alley, a terrain defined by the lack of mobility of its residents. Scarface—formerly of the Geto Boys—underscores this point on the single "On My Block," where he rhymes, "It's like the rest of the world don't exist/We stay confined to the same spot we been livin' in."*[10]

Cobb's framing is a burgeoning concept in hip-hop studies, as scholars and cultural critics are now considering how regional and local (and, in a broader sense, international) space and place coalesce to form hip-hop culture. Murray Forman (*The 'Hood Comes First: Race, Space, and Place in Rap and Hip-Hop* [2002]) and Mickey Hess (*Is Hip Hop Dead?: The Past, Present, and Future of America's Most Wanted Music* [2007] and *Hip Hop in America: A Regional Guide* [2010]) together have done the most significant work in pushing the concept of space and place in hip-hop, and this investigation of Houston's hip-hop uses their theories as a model.[11]

As such, understanding the local and regional spaces and places that commingle to form hip-hop culture is important because hip-hoppers, particularly rappers, narrate the life experiences of those from their locality—often presenting a counter narrative to American exceptionalism. Tangential to this, rappers communicate to the world the general social norms and cultural nuances of their place. Also, hip-hoppers express their identities through allegiances to a local space, and in doing so the rapper often becomes the center of the world, explaining his or her worldview from a local domain. Yet these places are not closed off so that participators can't leave and others can't come in; people take place particulars with them when leaving, and others enter with their own experiences. Next, local and regional production typically occurs within a close-knit team operating on independent labels due in large part to the distance separating them from major labels and major label respect. Lastly, rappers get their start and earn their stripes in their local place before getting the opportunity to represent on a larger stage—if not, their authenticity, which is the central ethos of hip-hop culture, is questioned. It is these local particulars and expressions that make hip-hop culture a special hybrid.[12]

To the point about where and how rappers get their start, Murray Forman claimed:

> *Few rap scholars and* [music critics] *(Tricia Rose and Brian Cross being notable exceptions) have paid attention to these formative stages and the slow processes of developing MC and DJ skills. There is, in fact, a trajectory to an artist's development that is seldom accounted for. In practice, artists' lyrics and rhythms must achieve success on the home front first, where the flow, subject matter, style and image must resonate meaningfully among those who share common bonds to place, to the posse and to the hood. In this sense, when rappers refer to the "local flavor," they are identifying the detailed inflections that respond to and reinforce the significance of the music's particular sites of origin and which might be recognized by others elsewhere as being unique, interesting and, ultimately, marketable.*[13]

Forman's argument is particularly evident in the lack of thorough investigation of Houston's hip-hop culture. Critics have overwhelmingly begun their investigations of Houston's hip-hop culture with the founding of Rap-A-Lot Records (1986) and the products of its most famous group, the Geto Boys. In contrast, their investigations of East Coast (particularly New York) and West Coast (particularly Los Angeles and Compton) hip-hop development typically begin prior to the professionalization of the culture within those places.

Any historical analysis of Houston's hip-hop culture is severely flawed if the events and people who unintentionally began creating and participating in the culture are not investigated or discussed. Starting at the point of Houston's professionalization of its local hip-hop culture creates a schism in the historical body because it says that the culture that formed prior to professionalization was irrelevant and had no significant influence. Starting at that point also furthers a "single origin" and modulation narrative of hip-hop culture.

I argue that although hip-hop culture in Houston, unlike New York and Los Angeles, has received inadequate attention and recognition, it is a significant center of hip-hop culture. The early history of Houston's hip-hop culture provides candid insight into how young people from marginalized conditions—specifically African Americans—effectively diagnosed their social ills and expressed themselves during times of boom and bust in Houston. By not giving Houston hip-hop culture the attention it deserves, one generalizes hip-hop cultural development by assuming that hip-hop in Houston developed in the same way it did in other sites, ignores the contribution that hip-hoppers in Houston made to the broader culture and misses how Houstonians specifically participated in the hip-hop culture that came from New York and how they adapted hip-hop to fit their specific needs.

Houston's rich and unique hip-hop culture began in the early 1980s. It is most notably recognized by the music that came from artists (and groups) such as the Geto Boys, Scarface, UGK (Bun B and Pimp C), Gangsta N-I-P, DJ Screw, Lil' Flip, Slim Thug, Paul Wall, Mike Jones and Chamillionaire. As noted by Jamie Lynch, a chronicler of Houston hip-hop, "business wise, Houston's rap artists and label owners created a business model that often emphasized local sales over national exposure."[14]

In the mid-1980s, Houston was a major participant in hip-hop culture prior to showcasing its own artists and styles. Houston clubs were able to hold thousands of people in one spot to party to the latest hip-hop, and according to one of Houston's hip-hop pioneers, Steve Fournier, Houston was one of the largest consumer markets for rap records.[15] Further, Houston was home to Kidz Jamm, one of the first radio programs dedicated solely to hip-hop, which aired every Saturday morning from 1982 to 2005.

In terms of success, in 1991, the Geto Boys single "Mind Playing Tricks on Me" reached number one on the Billboard Hot Rap Singles and number ten on the Billboard Hot R&B/Hip-Hop Songs. Two years following the

Geto Boys' chart success, UGK's single "Pocket Full of Stones" was featured on the soundtrack to the popular 1993 movie *Menace II Society*. UGK's fourth album, *Ridin' Dirty* (1996), reached number two on the Billboard Top R&B/Hip-Hop Albums and number fifteen on the Billboard 200. Lil' Flip's second studio album, *U Gotta Feel Me* (2004), debuted at number four on the Billboard 200 list. Scarface's album *The Fix* (2002) and Bun B's *Trill OG* (2010) both received the coveted "Five Mic Album" recognition from *The Source* magazine. In 2005, Mike Jones sold 1 million records (platinum) during the first week of his debut album *Who Is Mike Jones?* In addition, Chamillionaire's song "Ridin'" was the most popular ringtone download in 2006, with 3.2 million downloads. In the first five years of the twenty-first century, hip-hop artists and other entertainers flocked to Houston to get their custom-made grills from Paul Wall. And the innovations of DJ Screw's chopped and screwed techniques can be found on most popular hip-hop and R&B songs of the day.

Despite these successes and Houston's contribution to hip-hop culture, much of what is understood about Houston hip-hop is superficial, distorted and sometimes downright disrespectful. This study helps to fill that void by examining the early history of hip-hop in Houston. With this in mind, this text will describe and analyze the development of the culture, the nature of the culture and the impact of the culture by answering six specific questions: (1) Is Houston a music city—and if so, what African American music traditions existed in Houston prior to hip-hop? (2) Why is Houston's hip-hop culture unrecognized or underreported in scholarly and journalistic critiques? (3) How did hip-hop culture arrive in Houston? (4) What were the social, spatial and political contexts that allowed for the development of Houston's hip-hop culture? (5) How did Houstonians begin to participate in and appropriate hip-hop culture? (6) What role did Rap-A-Lot Records and the Geto Boys play in bringing early national attention to Houston's hip-hop culture?

The years including and in between 1979 and 1991 are important to proving the aforementioned claims and in answering these questions because they both represent turning points in hip-hop cultural history. After 1979, hip-hop went from a local/regional esoteric expression to a national phenomenon and commercial opportunity. In the same way, after 1991, Houston, because of the chart success of the Geto Boys' single "Mind Playing Tricks on Me," earned a spot, in terms of rank legitimacy, on the hip-hop map.

This investigation relied heavily on oral history interviews and song lyrics as primary sources. The oral histories were very important in telling this story because the documentation covering the early years of Houston's hip-hop culture is limited. Further, most of the individuals who played a role in developing the culture are still alive and as such can provide firsthand knowledge of the culture's ascent. Interviews were conducted with club and radio DJs, artists, club owners, promoters, record shop workers and lay historians. Song lyrics were examined to understand the nature of the music that came from the culture and to also understand the life experiences of those who created the music. Other sources consulted include music reviews, local and national periodicals that covered Houston hip-hop culture and books explaining Houston's musical traditions. Also surveyed were various texts that explore hip-hop culture and those that explain African American music and literary traditions.

When I began this project, I was reminded of popular biblical narrative found in John 1:46, which recounts a conversation between one of Jesus's new converts, Philip, and Nathanael. In this scripture, Nathanael contests the messianic nature of Jesus upon hearing that Jesus's place of origin was Nazareth—a place of low prominence and ill repute. Nathanael was noted as saying, "Nazareth? Can anything good come from there?"[16] In response to Nathanael's bemusement and doubt, Phillip says, "Come and see!"[17] In like manner, this project has the same aim: to elucidate on hip-hop culture from a place not regarded for its artistic products or as a hip-hop city. The story herein offers a cultural history of Houston, using hip-hop as its subject matter to redress the biases against Houston's hip-hop culture, to give identity to and show the agency of Houston's hip-hoppers and to analyze the ways in which members of Houston's hip-hop generation used hip-hop to comment on and become part of the American Dream.

chapter 1
FROM GOOD LIL' HOOD THING TO A NATIONAL PHENOMENON

HIP-HOP'S EARLY DEVELOPMENT AND EXPANSION

This history begins as another is ending. The first story is full of optimism and exalted ideas about humanity's ability to change through political action and moral argument. The next story, the plot we're living right now, is defined by cynicism, sarcasm, and self-involvement raised to art. The starting point was the early '70s.
—Nelson George, 2005[18]

Although hip-hop culture cannot be understood without the geographical and cultural contexts that contributed and still contribute to its overall ethos, it must first be understood from its original place and practices. Only then can one understand how hip-hop arrived in Houston and how Houston became a significant hip-hop place.

Hip-hop culture, like other cultures, is shared by a particular group of people, during a particular time, with its members responding to nature by classifying and encoding their experiences using particular forms—graphic arts, literature, fashion, dance, language, film, collective ideologies and music. The most popular expressive form of hip-hop culture is music, and its most common genre is known as rap (which is often inappropriately used interchangeably with the phrase hip-hop). Its exact date of birth cannot actually be determined; however, scholars and laymen both agree that its public debut occurred in the early 1970s on the streets of the Bronx.

For the most part, cultures are not intentionally created. They become cultures when customs and artifacts are passed through a group of people and from generation to generation. Cultural formation can be understood as accidental and responsive and as an antecedent of other cultures. Therefore, scholars and cultural critics have argued that hip-hop culture developed as a convergence of something accidental and responsive by youth within the urban underclass toward the social and political nature of American life at the beginning of the 1970s.[19]

Hip-hop culture was an accidental development; the young people who began hip-hopping in the Bronx did not suddenly decide to start a new culture. Hip-hop's accidental emergence was symbolic of a confluence of certain socio-political-technological phenomena that young people in the post-industrial Bronx initially responded to by partying to the cacophony of breakbeats, tagging subway trains and dancing. Nelson George proclaimed, "Hip-hop didn't start as a career move [or as a culture], but as a way of announcing one's existence to the world."[20] But why did these young people need to announce their existence to the world? What were their existential realities?

Hip-hop was a responsive development, because the young people who began hip-hopping in the Bronx were attempting to express and entertain themselves in the midst of scarcity and marginalization. Tricia Rose, pioneering scholar on hip-hop culture, argued that hip-hop was a way for the young people to negotiate their personal, economic and cultural realities in the face of deindustrialization.[21]

Rose and other scholars/cultural critics have also contended that one way that hip-hop developed was as a response from the dispossessed to a combination of several situations gone bad: post-industrialization, urban renewal, red-lining, access to and mass consumption of narcotics (namely, heroin and, later, crack cocaine), massive unemployment, increased crime and licentiousness and benign neglect.[22] These claims—although they may be uncomfortable to hear and politically charged—like the culture they represent, offer a counter narrative to American history in the last thirty years of the twentieth century. Ironically, it was these same situations that gave hip-hoppers something to talk about and led to entirely new income streams for young men and women from marginalized communities.

These young people were members of a shutout class that did not greatly benefit from the civil rights battles fought by some of their middle-class kin. Nelson George claimed that the story of these people, specifically young people in the Bronx and other post-industrial cities, is not often communicated because they represent America's dark history.[23]

Hip-hop pioneer Melle Mel provided a poignant analysis of the pitiful state of the post-industrial Bronx in his notable recording "The Message"

(1982).[24] His diagnosis of the post-industrial Bronx lyrically represented some of the socio-political issues that the young people in the Bronx began responding to.[25] George argued that, "Behind the decay and neglect, the place [the Bronx] was a cauldron of vibrant, unnoticed, and quite visionary creativity born of its racial mix and its relative isolation. It was within its boundaries that the expressions we associate with hip hop—graffiti art, break dancing, MCing, and mixing—all have roots."[26] Mark Anthony Neal championed the idea that they began to "narrate, critique, challenge and deconstruct the realities of postindustrial life."[27] Using new technology and appropriating antecedent cultural forms, these young people developed a new social and expressive movement.

Like other cultural developments, hip-hop borrowed from antecedent cultural forms—it sampled from so many expressions to make its own stance in the world. Music journalist John F. Szwed asked two important questions about hip-hop's origins: "Does rap have a beginning?" and "Where does the credit or (some might say) the blame lie?"[28] Szwed argued that things in American culture are not as pure as they claim to be. He claimed that we borrow from each other, appropriating what we have learned from other cultures to fit our own needs.

Although hip-hop was a new public culture that hit America by storm in the early 1980s, its early development and subsequent transformations are somewhat antecedent forms appropriated to fit the needs of the hip-hop generation. Rap, a form of music and talk, shares kinship with children's counting chants, cadence counting chants, military drills, work songs, tobacco auctioneers, "singing the word" preaching style, toasting, spoken-word poetry and rhyming DJs.[29]

In America, graffiti began to pop up after World War I on boxcars and subways as a way of marking one's appearance in a particular place or to express one's love. In the late 1960s, writing or spraying on clean edifices was used by urban youth to announce themselves to the world on burnt-out buildings and subway cars in cities like Philadelphia, New York City and Los Angeles. This appropriation of an old art became viewed as public nuisance because it went against the public narratives of America the beautiful.[30]

Hip-hop's original dance—break dancing—was an appropriation of antecedent forms that Jorge "Popmaster Fable" Pabon identified as:

> *Uprocking, tap, lindy hop, James Brown's good foot, salsa, Afro-Cuban, and various African and Native American dances. There's even a top-rock Charleston step called the "Charlie Rock!" Early influences on b-boying*

and b-girling also included martial arts films from the 1970s. Certain moves and styles developed form this inspiration.[31]

Hip-hoppers appropriated these forms as ways of competition and to express individuality, both essential tenets of hip-hop.

This new expressive culture—accidental, responsive and an appropriation of antecedent forms—became hip-hop, with four initial conduits of expression: (1) DJing, (2) graffiti, (3) break dancing/b-boying and (4) emceeing/rapping. As noted previously, some of hip-hop's practices existed in African American and Caribbean urban communities for years, but hip-hop represented the initial public offering of these communal experiences. Hip-hop culture is now represented by many other forms of expression, including fashion, cinematography, journalism, political thought and academic scholarship. But in context of this analysis, Houstonians began to appropriate and add to the initial forms of expression.

DISK JOCKEYING:
THE INSTRUMENTAL ELEMENT OF HIP-HOP CULTURE

In the late 1960s and early 1970s, mobile disc jockeys in the Bronx began transporting their turntables, big speaker systems and large record collections to dilapidated project parks. These mobile DJs had a new technology called the "mixer." The mixer allowed DJs to make seamless transitions between songs and to keep the music continuous, whereas before there would be a gap in between songs. The *Encyclopedia of Rap and Hip Hop Culture* defined the mixer as follows:

> *The core of the traditional DJ setup, the mixer, provides a way to set the levels between different audio sources. Without it, hip-hop DJing could not [have] developed as it has. Before the invention of the cross fader, DJs had to use two hands to move sound between the two turntables, using the volume control. With the cross fader, the DJ needs only one hand and can use the free hand to perform techniques such as backspinning, cutting, scratching, mixing, blending, and punch-phrasing.*[32]

The most notable mobile DJs that distinguished mixing were DJ Kool Herc, Afrika Bambaataa and Grandmaster Flash. DJs are important to the development of hip-hop culture because they made the music through reinterpretation of antecedent and shared music forms, they gave the music its sound, they broke new music and they introduced the world to the emcee/rapper, the role in hip-hop culture that would become the most notable representation of the culture.

Using music from multiple genres, DJs (with DJ Kool Herc being the innovator) began extending the breakbeats of songs for the crowd to dance to and later for the rapper to rap to. A breakbeat is "the drum solo in funk, R&B, soul, rock, jazz fusion, or other music."[33] This extension of the breakbeats was a reinterpretation of older forms of music and thus a new way to make music, especially in a live setting.

Herc also utilized big speaker systems to propagate the music farther into the eardrums of listeners, chakras of dancers and through the apartments in the neighborhood. His "were more powerful than the average DJ's speakers and surprisingly free of distortion, even when played outdoors. They produced powerful bass frequencies and played clear treble ones."[34] This was something that he may have appropriated from his Jamaican roots.

Two other innovations signify the role of the disc jockey in the development of hip-hop culture. The first was that of "scratching," which was created by the Grand Wizard Theodore but sustained and made popular by Grandmaster Flash. The second was backspinning. Rose defined both:

> *Scratching is a turntable technique that involves playing the record back and forth with your hand by scratching the needle against and then with the groove. Using two turntables, one record is scratched in rhythm or against the rhythm of another record while a second record played. This innovation extended Kool Herc's use of turntables as talking instruments and exposed the cultural rather than structural parameters of accepted turntable use.*

> *Backspinning allows the DJ to "repeat phrases and beats from a record by rapidly spinning it backwards." Employing exquisite timing, these phrases could be repeated in varying rhythmic patterns, creating the effect of a record skipping irregularly or a stutter effect, building intense crowd participation. Breakbeats were particularly good for building new compositions.*[35]

Rose reasoned that Afrika Bambaataa's contribution is an extension of what Herc did in that he began using "beats from European disco bands such as Kraftwerk, rock, and soul in his performances."[36] Bambaataa also used his role of disc jockey to unite his community, which was overrun by gangs and gang activities. He founded the Zulu Nation, "a collection of DJs, breakers, graffiti artists, and homeboys that filled the fraternal role gangs play in urban culture while de-emphasizing crime and fighting."[37]

In the mid- to late 1970s, DJs began to control sections of their community, and no other DJ could come into a specific community because the hip-hoppers had loyalty to their local DJ. DJs also began battling each other to show their prowess on the wheels of steel and to claim the throne of "Best DJ." There were DJ crews that served as constructive alternatives to gangs. The music that the DJs created became popular, so DJs began making mixtapes that spread through the boroughs, to other states and, later, overseas on military bases and on Caribbean islands.[38]

Soon, DJs began to employ the lyrical skills of an emcee to hype the crowd, announce the next party or toast. The emcee rapped to the beat using call-and-response to get the audience engaged, and together the DJ, the emcee and the audience became participants in the entire expression. This addition of an emcee was an extension of a concept developed by black radio DJs in the 1940s:

> Beginning in the 1940s, black radio DJs demonstrating their verbal dexterity on the air were, in some respects, the precursors to modern rap stars. Using the latest bebop slang and the storytelling traditions of African Americans, DJs, such as Chicago's Al "The Midnight Gambler" Benson and Dr. Hepcat of Austin, Texas, promoted records and products using hip rhymes and melodic chatter. The preeminent DJ of the era was New York City's Douglas "Jocko" Henderson. Henderson's "Ace of Rockets" radio show not only influenced other American DJs but also was instrumental in the development of hip-hop via the Caribbean.[39]

As emcees gained more popularity, their lyrical skills were highly demanded. These emcees began to record tapes of themselves rhyming over the beat or over a DJ's mix and then began to pass the tapes out around their communities. These emcees also handed their tapes over to DJs so that the DJ could advertise for the emcee. The DJ, thus, broke new music. This would lead to the advent of the rapper and the spread of rap music.

GRAFFITI:
THE GRAPHIC ART ELEMENT OF HIP-HOP CULTURE

Historically considered a nuisance, graffiti was a medium for marginalized young people to come to the center by using spray paints and the felt-tipped pen. Graffiti artists used buildings, subway trains, buses and almost anything as a canvas to announce a party, a warning, their place in the world or their community. There were early developments of hip-hop graffiti in Philadelphia through the works of Cornbread and Top Cat, who later moved to New York. But in media discourse, New York graffiti gained the most attention because of the local government's relentless maneuvers to erase graffiti from all public edifices and get rid of all of the graffiti "artists."

Craig Castleman chronicled the rise and tensions of the graffiti culture in New York in his essay entitled "The Politics of Graffiti." Castleman noted that the *New York Times* began covering graffiti in 1971 because of the reoccurring presence of a tag that read "Taki 183." The first article was entitled "'Taki 183' Spawns Pals," and it helped to familiarize New Yorkers with graffiti, much to the chagrin of the Metro Transit Authority and Mayor John V. Lindsay. Graffiti became a major problem for New York, as the city spent millions of dollars to clean subways and buildings and deter graffiti activity.[40]

Rose argued that graffiti was significant to the development of hip-hop culture because "by the mid-1970s, graffiti took on a new focus and complexity." Taggers began to appropriate graffiti by developing their own styles. She continued her argument, claiming that "small-scale tagging developed into the top to bottom, a format that covered a section of a train car from the roof to the floor. This was followed by the top to bottom whole car and multiple car 'pieces,' an abbreviation for graffiti master pieces."[41] In the process, graffiti became the art of hip-hop culture.

BREAK DANCING/B-BOYS AND B-GIRLS:
THE DANCE ELEMENT OF HIP-HOP CULTURE

Break dancing combines "a medley of moves adapting a number of sources—the shuffling, sliding steps of James Brown; the dynamic, platformed dancers on Don Cornelius's syndicated *Soul Train* television show; Michael Jackson's robotic moves that accompanied the 1974 hit 'Dancin' Machine' and the athletic whips and spins of kung fu movies—all of which were funneled through the imagination of black New Yorkers."[42] Break dancing was first used to squash gang beefs between black New York gangs and then made popular and competitive by young Puerto Rican communities. Break dancing—like other dance movements created by people of color—defied Puritanical standards of dance and used the body in a way to say something political.

Kool Herc noticed that the young people at his parties would perform unique dances to his extended breakbeats, and he soon began to call these dancers b-boys (break boys). These b-boys (and girls) became regular features at Herc's parties and other parties across the boroughs. Often, their dancing was led by instructions from guys talking over the beats: emcees.

THE EMCEE AND RAPPER: THE ORAL ELEMENT OF HIP-HOP CULTURE

Rap music is hip-hop culture's most expressive and popular form. Rose asserted, "Rap is a complex fusion of orality and postmodern technology."[43] The oral part of rap is an extension of African and African American oral and literary traditions. "Rap lyrics invoke and revise stylistic and thematic elements that are deeply wedded to a number of black cultural storytelling forms, most prominently toasting and the blues."[44] Also, rap has its roots in Negro spirituals, slave songs and the storytelling of the African griot. In the *Norton Anthology of African American Literature*, Henry Louis Gates proclaimed:

> *Rap draws from such varied sources as jump-rope rhymes and other game changes and songs; competitive trickster's toasts and badman boasts such as those of Stackolee and Shine; chanted sermons of black churches (including those of the Nation of Islam); the scat singing of jazz musicians such as Louis Armstrong and Cab Calloway; "vocalese" jazz singing (fitting words and scat phrases to recorded jazz solos); favorite radio disc-jockey's patter; and the widely popular Black Arts movement poetry of such writers as Nikki Giovanni, Amiri Baraka, Jayne Cortez, Gil Scott-Heron, and the Last Poets—the latter, in turn, influenced by the poetry of Langston Hughes, Sterling Brown, and other black poets working (in the circling pattern of influence so typical of the arts in America) in a black vernacular idiom.*[45]

The lyrics can be boastful, comedic, tragicomedy, documentarian, conscious, horror-themed, something to dance to, misogynistic or even pornographic. Borrowing from African and African American oral traditions, rappers signify, boast, brag, fib, rhyme, symbolize; use metaphor and simile, onomatopoeia, irony and personification; and dramatize to tell real and surreal stories of American life—especially the stories of those in marginalized communities in America.

Structurally, a rap song contains poetry spoken over syncopated rhythms within musical bars. The rapper raps the song with style and flow. Mtume Ya Salaam reasoned:

> *Style refers both to the tonal quality in a rapper's vocals and to the level of originality in presentation and delivery. Flow describes a rapper's sense of rhythm and timing. The concept of flow differentiates rap music from other music with spoken lyrics (for example, the music of Gil Scott-Heron, The Last Poets, or even Cab Calloway). Rap lyrics are delivered in a rhythmic cadence, not simply recited or melodically half-sung.*[46]

Although rap is an extension of African and African American oral traditions, rap relies heavily on technology. Rap needs mixers, samplers and a microphone. All of these tools—as well as rapper's lyrics—give the song meaning. In the absence of technology, a beatboxer created the sounds (breakbeats, scratching and backspins) and samples that DJs normally provided.[47]

In its hip-hop form, rapping took place in neighborhood parks, on street corners or in homes where young men and women practiced their techniques. After practicing, they tested their skills by battling at a club, house party, basketball game or in the courtyard of the projects. Soon, music producers saw that they could profit from the growing trend. The commoditization of this street phenomenon brought the emcee from the background to the center of hip-hop culture.

HIP-HOP'S TIPPING POINTS

The first tipping point came in 1979, when the Sugar Hill Gang—a mix of young rappers from Englewood, New Jersey, brought together in the form of a group by producer and Sugar Hill label owner Sylvia Robinson—gained

It ["Rapper's Delight"] was something different...[it was] easy to mimic, easy to remember. It was something catchy.—Sire Jukebox[51]

"Rapper's Delight" was the first rap song that people knew word for word. It had cross-genre appeal. People who loved rock-and-roll knew "Rapper's Delight." People who liked country knew "Rapper's Delight." It sort of bridged the gap between rap being taboo and rap being socially acceptable.— Luscious Ice[52]

I was nine years old when "Rapper's Delight" came out. It blew everybody's mind because at the time, rap was something relatively new. Also, all we jammed was the Isley Brothers, Al Green and all of the R&B legends. But when this new thing came in, when these guys were rapping, it messed everybody's head up. It took everybody by storm—even the adults were drawn into it. I can recall... memorizing every word.—K-Rino[53]

huge popularity. The group caught national attention when they interpolated Chic's song "Good Times" on their rap song "Rapper's Delight." Though not the first hip-hop record, this was the first hip-hop record to go mainstream. According to Rose, "By early 1980, 'Rapper's Delight' had sold several million copies and risen to the top of the pop charts."[48] The Sugar Hill Gang signed a record deal, performed internationally and was seen on TV across the world. Mickey Hess revealed that a "St. Louis radio DJ, Gentleman Jim Gates, was the first DJ to play 'Rapper's Delight' on the radio."[49] This was considered a defining moment in hip-hop culture, as it has "been cited by rappers all over the country as their first encounter with hip hop's sound and style."[50]

After "Rapper's Delight," more albums received commercial success across the country. Rose noted:

Within the next three years Kurtis Blow's "The Breaks," Spoonie Gee's "Love Rap," The Treacherous Three's "Feel the Heartbeat," Afrika Bambaataa and the Soul Sonic Force's "Planet Rock," Sequence's "Funk You Up" and Grandmaster Flash and the Furious Five's "The Message" were commercially marketed and successful rap singles.[54]

During the next few years, radio stations in New York, Philadelphia, Los Angeles and the Bay Area began to play rap music. Popular radio programs included Mr. Magic's Rap Attack, which was "the first regularly scheduled rap music program in the nation"; DJ Red Alert's show on WBLS-FM; and KDAY-1580 AM with Greg Mack.[55] Along with radio stations playing rap music, a few music video shows began to sprout up. In New York, there was Video Music Box. These mediums helped people across the nation connect to hip-hop culture and influenced many to participate.

As hip-hop became more popular in the early 1980s, films, news coverage and television shows about it cropped up to explain the culture to a broader audience. These visual media outlets were played across the country and exposed hip-hop culture to adults and kids alike:

1981—ABC's *20/20* airs "Rappin' to the Beat," television's first national news story on hip-hop.[56]

1982—Premier of Charlie Ahearn's *Wild Style*, the first feature film about hip-hop culture.[57] The film depicted hip-hop culture elements by the people who were involved in the beginnings of the culture: Fab 5 Freddy, the Rock Steady Crew, the Cold Crush Brothers, etc.

1984—Henry Chalfant and Tony Silver's *Style Wars*, the first documentary about hip-hop culture, was broadcast on PBS.[58]

1984—Premier of *Beat Street*, directed by Stan Lathan. In 1984, *New York Times* writer Vincent Canby noted, "[The movie] is designed for everybody who still hasn't had his or her fill of break dancing, or who doesn't yet understand that break dancing, rap singing and graffiti are legitimate expressions of the urban artistic impulse."[59]

1984—Premier of *Breakin'*, a film based in Los Angeles that paired street break-dancers with a jazz dancer. The film was a West Coast offering of hip-hop culture, specifically break dancing. It was also the acting debut of rapper Ice-T.

1985—Michael Schultz's *Krush Groove*, featuring performances by Run-D.M.C., the Fat Boys, L.L. Cool J, Kurtis Blow and the Beastie Boys and made on a $3 million budget, opened in 515 theaters nationwide and was cited as the number-one movie in America by *Variety* the following week.[60]

1985—Brought to the screens by Barry Gordy, *The Last Dragon* was a kung-fu flick infused with hip-hop. The movie featured break dancing, graffiti, rapping and other motifs from hip-hop culture. It became a cult classic.

Another catalyst for the spread of hip-hop culture came in 1984 when Swatch Watch sponsored Swatch Watch New York City Fresh Fest. The tour featured acts like Run-D.M.C., Kurtis Blow, Whodini, the Fat Boys, Newcleus and New York's Dynamic Breakers. George reported:

> *These stadium-size gigs allowed performers to proselytize like hip-hop evangelists. Kids in D.C., where go-go was the local music, and in Oakland, with its rich and varied culture, and Los Angeles, where a mobile post-disco party scene was thriving, came to see the Kings from Queens* [Run-D.M.C.]. *Not only were they converted as listeners— many customers came away convinced they could perform too.*[61]

John Nova Lomax reported:

> *K-Rino* [a Houston rapper] *became a lifelong rap junkie at the Southern Star Amphitheater* [at Astroworld] *in the mid-80s. The Fresh Fest, a package tour with headliners Run-D.M.C., L.L. Cool J, and the Fat Boys and "all them cats that was in the movie* Krush Groove*" pushed him over the edge. "Man, it was packed," he says. "Watching it, I was like, 'Man, I got to be that person one day that's up there.'"*[62]

With the commercial success of "Rapper's Delight," the advent of radio and video shows, hip-hop films and documentaries and the Swatch Watch New York City Fresh Fest, hip-hop became national. Young people across the country wanted to be hip-hoppers, including the country kids in Houston, Texas.

Hip-Hop Historiography

Within ten years of hip-hop's public debut, scholars and cultural critics began to investigate hip-hop as an academic subject and culture. The rise of hip-hop studies came as an intervention in the wake of alarming attacks on, misunderstanding of and underreporting on the culture, and as members of the hip-hop generation came of age and wanted to give voice and a historical narrative to their culture. Studies from Tricia Rose (*Black Noise: Rap Music and Black Culture in Contemporary America*), Robin D.G. Kelley (*Race Rebels: Culture, Politics, and the Black Working Class*), and William Perkins (*Droppin'*

Science: Critical Essays on Rap Music and Hip-Hop Culture) were some of the first scholarly considerations of hip-hop culture, and they offered excellent critiques and historical contexts of hip-hop culture that set the precedent for other scholars to follow.

Throughout the 1990s and during the early years of the 2000s, journalists and scholars alike endeavored to write general histories of hip-hop culture. Notable works include Nelson George's *Hip-Hop in America* (1998), David Toop's *Rap Attack 3* (2000), Alex Ogg and David Upshal's *The Hip-Hop Years: A History of Rap* (2001) and Jeff Chang's *Can't Stop Won't Stop: A History of the Hip-Hop Generation* (2005). These general or universal attempts of historization contextualized hip-hop culture where misunderstanding existed, but none went deep into regional and local sites, thus denying agency and identity to local hip-hoppers and neglecting the contribution that these sites made to the overall culture and the ways in which people in these sites hip-hopped.

The aforementioned scholars and cultural critics employed several interdisciplinary methods to define and bring to fore the life, cultural practices, politics, aesthetics and voice of hip-hop culture and those within the hip-hop generation. Moreover, they attempted to present a counter narrative on the last quarter of the twentieth century in America. Yet out of the exigencies to give identity and agency to the culture and people, they presented universalized or "single origin" narratives of hip-hop culture.

To date, much of hip-hop historiography was presented as and often viewed as a national "imagined community."[63] Murray Forman argued in his article "Represent: Race, Space and Place in Rap Music" that "over the years [of hip-hop reporting]…there has been little attention granted to the implications of hip-hop's spatial logics." He continued to argue, in referring to an article from *Time* magazine entitled "Hip-Hop Nation: After 20 Years—How It's Changed America" that "*Time*'s coverage is relatively standard in perceiving the hip-hop nation as a historical construct rather than a geo-cultural amalgamation of personages and practices that are spatially dispersed."[64] This universalizing of hip-hop declared East Coast (New York boroughs and Philadelphia) and West Coast (Los Angeles and Compton) hip-hop culture as the essential identities and representations of hip-hop culture and all other sites as consumers or modulations.

The narratives that buttressed the singular and universal historization of hip-hop culture at the same time unconsciously "otherized" everything else. Hence, rappers and critics were able to claim the death of hip-hop when it did not sound like, look like or act like East Coast or West Coast hip-hop. They overlooked how hip-hop affected those in regional and local communities. Further, general histories of hip-hop culture dismissed the contributions of hip-hoppers from regional and local areas, especially from the South.[65] Ironically, southern blues, funk and soul music provided much of the instrumentation that underlay the lyrics of many hip-hop songs. In addition, southern hip-hop dominated the airwaves and sales of hip-hop music for much of the late 1990s into the 2000s.[66]

Consequently, further examination of the nature of hip-hop was needed, particularly that which focused on regional and local studies of hip-hop culture. Regional and local studies of hip-hop culture attempted to investigate hip-hop culture from the bottom up, focusing on grassroots movements and juxtaposing the regional/local area with the national culture of hip-hop. Three texts standout for their innovative investigations of regional/local hip-hop sites: *Hip Hop in America: A Regional Guide* (edited by Mickey Hess, 2010), *Third Coast: OutKast, Timbaland, and How Hip-Hop Became a Southern Thing* (Roni Sarig, 2007) and *Dirty South: OutKast, Lil' Wayne, Soulja Boy, and the Southern Rappers Who Reinvented Hip-Hop* (Ben Westoff, 2011).[67] All three texts added much data and context to each region/locale of hip-hop culture. In particular, the work of Sarig and Westoff began a new trajectory in hip-hop studies with their regional investigations.

Although each attempted to tell "grassroots" hip-hop stories, all three failed to address the social and political realities of each locale, did not delve deep enough into the ways in which all people have experienced the culture, began their investigation at the professionalization of local hip-hop culture and relied heavily on secondary sources. Their works were mostly the stories of regional and local hip-hop heroes. This was definitely the case in their investigations of Houston's hip-hop culture.[68]

Journalist John Nova Lomax claimed that media began to pay more attention to Houston's hip-hop culture at the beginning of the twenty-first century because Houston artists began to dominate the airwaves and charts and because they were heavily influencing the culture.[69] However, reports on the culture often dismissed twenty years of history that contributed to the rise of Houston's hip-hop culture and focused on the big names, thus invalidating the roots and unknown pioneers.[70] In an interview with Lomax, rapper K-Rino expressed his discontent with that type of storytelling. Lomax reported:

> [K-Rino is] *not content to let revisionist history marginalize his clique's feats; MTV's Houston rap documentary failed to even mention SPC* [South Park Coalition]. *"They tryin' to write us out of history,"* he

says. "You hear about the Screwed Up Click, you hear about Swishahouse, you hear about Rap-A-Lot. You hear about all these different entities that played major roles and shaped the city, but they never mention us, and I've got a problem with that."[71]

To K-Rino's point, Houston's hip-hop culture did not start in 1986 when James Smith (James Prince or Lil' J) founded Rap-A-Lot Records, just as hip-hop culture did not begin in 1979 when the Sugar Hill Gang caught national attention with "Rapper's Delight." Both of these moments were more like tipping points rather than starting points. They are connected to stories that began a few years earlier—stories that began as something coincidental and later became intentional. Yet this is where the historization of Houston's hip-hop culture begins in most of the texts that have attempted to write about Houston. Why this limited scope? At least four plausible explanations exist:

1. The historical understandings of the South, in particular Texas and Houston, are marred by years of discourse that imagines the South as "country" and Houston (and Texas alike) as slow and backward, which suggests that nothing worthy of cultural critique could come from these places.[72]

2. The narrators of the hip-hop story have a nostalgia for hip-hop's early days on the East Coast and measure everything after those days as less than or "other."

3. These same narrators typically chronicled Houston's hip-hop story from a distance, as travelers, and covered only the common subjects.

4. No scholar from the hip-hop generation has attempted to tell the Houston hip-hop story.

Fittingly, in March 2013, Beyoncé released an edgy, braggadocios song titled "Bow Down/I Been On," a two-part song on which she unapologetically claimed queen status ("Bow Down") and represented Houston's hip-hop particulars ("I Been On"). Upon release, the song and Beyoncé were slammed by many critics because of her use of the word "bitch" ("Bow Down") and for the style and content chosen ("I Been On," chopped and screwed). Most of the critiques lacked context, particularly the space and place contexts that shaped Beyoncé—Houston's hip-hop culture. In response to the critiques and as a way to pay further homage to Houston,

Beyoncé recruited rappers Bun B, Scarface, Willie D, Lil' Keke and Z-Ro to create a remix to the "I Been On" part of the song. In each of the rappers' verses, they boldly professed and chronicled Houston's hip-hop history and reminded anyone who would hate that Houston has been on—that is that Houston is not new to the hip-hop game and should not be taken for granted. Scarface's verse perfectly elucidates this claim:

> *I been on, now who you goons gon' get to knock me off?*
> *I've been boss, been on slabs, been on paint*
> *Been on fours homey, I've been on drapes, I've been half-baked*
> *Twenty-five years and ain't fell off yet cause my flow that wet*
> *You don't want no plex, they talk that shit*
> *The Queen Bey said you better bow down, bitch.*

chapter 2
HOUSTON, A BLACK MUSIC CITY?

Houston is a camouflaged city when it comes to music. There's something there—but away from it, you can't really see it.
—James Bolden, 1998[73]

I s Houston a music city?

This is a question that a few people have attempted to answer to determine if Houston has a black music tradition worthy of national praise and critique. But more importantly, if it does have a black music tradition, what type of national impact has it made?

Before Houston became a hip-hop city, it was home to other black music traditions, namely blues, jazz, zydeco and gospel. Among these genres, the city, as professed by music critic David Nelson, is the "birthplace for 'some of the most significant developments in modern blues.'"[74] Even though these traditions date back to at least the beginning of the twentieth century and made major contributions to the nation, Nelson's kudos stand as a minority report, as Houston is still not regarded as a significant music city. One reason is that many music writers consistently search in the same places for the roots of certain music forms.[75]

Houston's isolation and independence also bear some of the blame for this under-recognition. While Houston is one of the largest and most populated cities in America, its distance from other major cities—New York, Los Angeles and Chicago—isolated it from prominent entertainment corporations, entertainment venues and those able to report on and consume its music. This isolation, consequently, positioned the city for successful developments, both business and cultural, independent of national support. Likewise, until they caught the attention of national artists or national record companies, Houston's black music artists had reasonable success performing for large local crowds in popular nightspots located in segregated wards and, sometimes, to white audiences. However, this isolation also prompted some of Houston's artists to depart for bigger lights where they were successful in other places like Los Angeles, New York, Chicago or New Orleans.

This disregard can also be attributed to Houston's endless desire to promote its bankable interests. As such, when one thinks of Houston's cultural contributions, three industries come to mind: oil and gas, healthcare and aerospace. In fact, Houston is considered the mecca for these industries. The Texas Medical Center, located in Houston, is the largest of its kind and known for its translational research, patient care and air ambulance system. People from around the globe travel to Houston to work in or do in business in the oil-and-gas industry. As far as space exploration, President John F. Kennedy promoted Houston as an aeronautical center in 1962 when he affirmed:

> *What was once the furthest outpost on the old frontier of the West will be the furthest outpost on the new frontier of science and space. Houston, your City of Houston, with its Manned Spacecraft Center, will become the heart of a large scientific and engineering community.*[76]

In full acceptance of our industry reputations, we branded our national sports teams in their honor—Oilers (former pro-football team), Astros (baseball), Rockets (basketball) and Aeros (hockey).[77] Accordingly, Houston, being the fourth-largest city in the United States, has promoted its reputation of technological and scientific genius—but definitely not music. Likewise, as Chris Gray argued, "Houston's ignorance of its rich musical history, willful or otherwise, has long been a sore spot for those of us who grow weary of crying out in the wilderness that there's more to this city than oil, hospitals, food and freeways."[78]

Still, another explanation deserves exploration because, for a time, scholarship chronicling the lives and contributions of Houston's African American culture was mediocre.[79] In the first three quarters of the twentieth century, many of those who did investigate the local history of Houston displayed their general ignorance and/or prejudices toward African

American stories and events. A cursory review of popular texts about Houston highlights the blatant oversight of racial minorities, in particular their cultural contributions.[80]

Beginning in the late 1970s and into the twenty-first century, scholars began to study and pen stories about Houston's African American cultural history. These works discussed the African American experience in Houston from exploration of the land to the mid-1980s, describing economic and social developments, community formations and characteristics, challenges with Jim Crow and housing problems and race relations.[81] Later commercial works highlighted civil rights battles from voting rights to desegregation of schools and public places; sit-ins led by Texas Southern University (TSU) students; political leaders such as Judson Robinson, Hattie Mae White, Barbara Jordan and Mickey Leland; University of Houston's first African American homecoming queen (Lynn Cecelia Eusan); athletic feats by George Foreman, Carl Lewis and many others; the first African American astronauts; and entertainment venues owned, operated and attended by African Americans.[82]

Yet for all of these strides to recover African American cultural history, music culture was left out. It took the work of Roger Wood to set the record straight. Wood undeniably substantiated Houston as a music city with deep black musical traditions in his three texts highlighting Houston's blues, jazz, zydeco and music production traditions: *Down in Houston: Bayou City Blues* (2003), *Texas Zydeco* (2006) and *House of Hits: The Story of Houston's Gold Star/ Sugar Hill Recording Studios* (2010).

In Wood's work, we find that Houston's black musical traditions began in the early part of the twentieth century, when large numbers of African Americans began migrating to Houston to take advantage of employment opportunities in the petrochemical industry, port jobs or other manufacturing opportunities. These early settlers brought their culture with them and settled in segregated wards. Wood argued, "The burgeoning numbers of new arrivals included many black Creoles from the prairies and bayous of nearby southwestern Louisiana, a cultural presence that has strongly flavored the development of African American music in Houston, especially blues-based forms."[83]

Along with the various ethnic and cultural strands that merged in Houston as a result of blacks' western migration, the city also received musical benefits because of its location. As the most populated city west of the Mississippi, Houston was a regional center for industry and entertainment. Scholar Garna L. Christian argued that because of this, black Houstonians were able to keep up with national trends:

Ragtime, in the form of marching bands, strutted in at the turn of the century. Minstrels, medicine shows, and circuses plied the area, constantly updating the community's musical awareness. In the wake of the Great War, Houston had its quota of establishments peddling prohibited booze and the newly named jazz, as the barrel-house piano gave ground to the clarinet, trumpet, and, ultimately, the saxophone as feature instruments. When the big band swing era took root during the Depression, local ballrooms and stage productions approximated the sounds of Duke Ellington, Jimmie Lunceford, and Artie Shaw. If a local band carved a niche, it could withstand the competition of nationally known groups, who routinely performed two-week stints in the years before jet transportation made one-nighters feasible. And just as local headliners trekked to the coasts to answer knocks of opportunity, incoming musicians left their tours to energize the Gulf Coast scene. Though known in the trade as something of a Friday and Saturday night town, Houston remained an important minor-league music center until World War II, when in the words of prominent bandleader [Conrad Johnson], *"Everything changed, and would never be the same."*[84]

At least until the late 1960s, Houston's African American culture developed and lived mainly within segregated communities—Third Ward, Fourth Ward, Fifth Ward, Sunnyside, Acreage Homes and South Park. Within these self-contained communities, vibrant cities within a city operated with separate medical facilities, schools, businesses and entertainment venues. Local artists cut their teeth in their own communities and then traveled with other national artists along the "chitlin' circuit," later recording their own music and gaining national acclaim. These segregated enclaves were the sites of origin for unique sounds and business models that eventually influenced hip-hop culture coming out of the same neighborhoods.[85]

JAZZ

Although no Texas city holds the rights to the "Texas sound," Houston, because of its artists, location and venues, contributed much to the Texas trajectory of jazz. Though there is no one point of origin, it can be argued that the culture was kick-started in the first three black high schools: Booker T. Washington, Phillis Wheatley and Jack Yates. The first generation of jazz artists to "make it" outside the city were trained in these schools—Milton Larkin (trumpet), Eddie "Cleanhead" Vinson (alto saxophone), Arnett Cobb (tenor saxophone), Illinois Jacquet (tenor saxophone), I.H. Smalley (clarinet and saxophone), Cedric Haywood (piano) and "Sonny Boy" Franklin (guitar). These and many other artists played in their schools' marching bands and often formed groups outside of school in which they performed in local clubs (Ethiopian Café and Harlem Grill) and at events to earn money.[86]

Initially, jazz was a hobby for them and a way to earn "pocket money," but at the point when many of them were getting ready to graduate or soon thereafter, it became a profession and a way of life. In 1936, Milton Larkin took over as bandleader at the Harlem Grill and recruited Cobb and Smalley as members of the house band. Larkin later added Jacquet, Vinson, Tom Archia (tenor saxophone), "Wild Bill" Davis (piano and organ) and Haywood to the band. This lineup played at local spots (black and white venues like the Eldorado Ballroom, the Empire Room, the Pilgrim Auditorium, the Majestic Theater and the Lincoln Theater) and also toured the country. Because of the success of these performances, the band and its individual members caught the attention of national stars. One such star was Lionel Hampton, who recruited Jacquet (1940) and Cobb (1942) to his orchestra.[87]

During and after the years of World War II, many of the musicians in this generation began to gain national attention from joining the bands of big stars, touring with their own bands and recording their own music. After Larkin's members left or were recruited by other bands, he entered the armed services, where he played in Sy Oliver's army band (1943–46). Larkin later recorded his own songs, played for a stint at Chicago's Rhumboogie Club and led a band in New York.[88] Vinson moved on to New York, where he began recording his own music (Mercury Records). He led his own band, which included a young John Coltrane, and his music also crossed over to blues. Jacquet found success recording with Hampton ("Flying Home"), starting his own band with his brother Russell Jacquet and Charles Mingus, playing with Count Basie, touring across the world and becoming the first artist-in-residence at Harvard University.[89] Cobb also recorded with Hampton, later formed his own band (1947) that toured the country until 1956, recorded his own songs, toured the world and at the end of his life founded the Texas Jazz Heritage Society. The successes from this generation of artists helped promote the "Texas sound" across the world.

Mention must also be made of Conrad Johnson. Johnson was an accomplished jazz musician and an even more accomplished teacher. He led the bands for Jack Yates, Booker T. Washington and, from 1957 to 1978, Kashmere. "His thirty-seven years of classroom service were highlighted by an amazing tenure as director of the Fifth Ward's Kashmere High School Stage Band—which won victories in forty-two out of forty-six festivals entered between 1969 and 1977, recorded eight albums featuring more than twenty original compositions by Johnson, and traveled throughout Europe, Japan, and the United States."[90] Johnson's pedagogy and mentoring helped to jump-start the careers of many jazz musicians from Houston, including Don Wilkerson, Sherman Robertson, Joe Carmouche and others. The feats by Conrad "Prof" Johnson and his stage band, Thunder Soul, were featured in a documentary produced by Jamie Foxx entitled *Thunder Soul* (2011).

Among this group of men, Houston ladies Sippie Wallace, Victoria Spivey, Daisy Richards (dancer) and Jewel Brown received particular national fame for their singing, most of which morphed into blues-style singing. Richards is famous for dancing or singing with Billie Holliday, Count Basie, Louis Jordan, Lena Horne, Pearl Bailey, Sarah Vaughan, Ella Fitzgerald and the Ink Spots. She also appeared on television with Milton Berle and Ed Sullivan.[91]

Spivey was a singer and songwriter who came to public attention in the late 1910s and early 1920s. During this time, she played in Lazy Daddy's Fillmore Blues Band (Dallas), L.C. Tolen's Band and Revue (Dallas) and also worked with Blind Lemon Jefferson. Spivey recorded with Okeh Records and in 1926 released her *Black Snake Blues*. She gained even more attention in 1929 for her role in the MGM King Vidor film *Hallelujah*, in which she played Missy Rose. Between 1926 and 1937, she wrote songs and recorded and/or performed with "Louis Armstrong, Henry Allen, Lee Collins, Lonnie Johnson, Memphis Minnie, Bessie Smith, and Tampa Red." In the 1960s, she created her own music label, Spivey Records. According to Donna Parker, in 1961, Spivey "produce[ed] her own recordings and those of other blues artists. One of her earliest releases was *Three Kings and the Queen* (1962), which included a young Bob Dylan on blues harmonica and backing vocals."[92]

Wallace, originally named Beulah Thomas, was born in Houston in 1898. She came from a family of singers and musicians (brothers George W. Thomas and Hersal Thomas and niece Hociel Thomas) who began their music careers at Shiloh Baptist Church. In 1915, Wallace moved to New Orleans with her brother Hersal Thomas to work with their older brother George Thomas (pioneer of the boogie-woogie piano style). There she was able to hone her craft working with some of New Orleans' rising stars, including King Oliver and Louis Armstrong. In 1923, she and Hersal moved to Chicago, and in quick time she signed a record deal with Okeh Records. Her recordings for Okeh were popular across the country, particularly her song "Shorty George Blues," which sold over 100,000 copies. Parker noted that Wallace was "promoted as the 'Texas Nightingale,'" and while an artist for Okeh, "she recorded more than forty songs…from 1924 to 1927 with such sidemen as Louis Armstrong, Johnny Dodds, Clarence Williams, and others."[93]

Wallace took a hiatus from blues recording for almost thirty-five years to take care of family members and also sing gospel music in her new home of Detroit. In the mid-1960s, she returned to blues performing and recording. In 1966, she recorded an album with Victoria Spivey titled *Sippie Wallace and Victoria Spivey*. According to Parker, Wallace's songs on this album fit perfectly into the rising feminist movement of the 1970s. At this time, Wallace's music also received renewed interest because of Bonnie Raitt, who revised two of Wallace's songs for her 1971 debut album. Raitt and Wallace later recorded and toured together. During the last years of her life, Wallace performed at the Lincoln Center and recorded a self-titled album, *Sippie* (1982).[94]

Brown has roots in Houston's blues but is most notably known as a jazz singer. Before graduating from Jack Yates, Brown was approached by Hampton to sing in his orchestra, but she turned him down. Brown left Houston in the late 1950s, and by 1957, she was performing in Los Angeles. She also worked in Dallas at the Sovereign Club managed by Jack Ruby. Brown's claim to fame came in 1961 when she became the lead vocalist for the Louis Armstrong All Star Band. She sang with Armstrong for seven years and then returned to Houston, where she retired for fifteen years. Brown came out of retirement in the 1980s and since has had a lucrative career recording and touring across the world. Most recently (2012), according to Wood, Brown collaborated with Houston Milton Hopkins (cousin of Sam "Lightnin'" Hopkins) on a highly acclaimed CD released by Austin-based Dialtone Records.

BLUES

According to Wood, "In the twenty-five years or so following the end of World War II, Houston was a place where African American musicians created some of the most influential blues-based music ever played, ranging from the down-home sounds of Lightnin' Hopkins to the more refined orchestrations of the Duke-Peacock recording empire and beyond."[95] Not only did the blues coming out of Houston achieve chart success, but it also inspired other artists' artistry. One such artist was England's own Richard Starkey, who became known to the world as Ringo Starr as a drummer and singer for the Beatles. While still a young lad (sixteen), Starr and a friend heard a recording of the music of Lightnin' Hopkins. They were so intrigued with his music that they attempted to get passports to move to Houston to be around Hopkins.[96]

Sam "Lightnin'" Hopkins was born Centerville, Texas, in 1912. He is one of the world's most beloved blues artists, and he called Houston home. He was mentored by two other blues greats: Alger "Texas" Alexander and Blind Lemon Jefferson. Hopkins spent his early life in and around Central and East Texas, where he picked cotton and sang and played the guitar for country parties and dances. As an irascible young adult, he found himself in many fights, which eventually led him to the chain gang. In his late twenties (around 1944–45), he and his wife moved to Houston, settling on Dowling Street in the Third Ward. Hopkins played at local juke joints, and in 1945, he recorded a few songs for a local label with Texas Alexander and Wilson "Thunder" Smith. A year later, he was "discovered" by Lola Anne Cullum, local talent scout, who drove Hopkins and Smith to Los Angles to record for Aladdin Records. Hopkins and Smith recorded eight to twelve titles for Aladdin under the name "Thunder Smith and Lightnin' Hopkins," among which "Katie Mae" became the most popular.[97] Although these songs were successful, Hopkins did not want to tour. He moved back to Houston, where he continued to perform in juke joints. In 1947, he began a two-year relationship with a local recording studio that was also home of the Gold Star Records label, with which he had much success from the songs "Short Haired Woman," "Baby Please Don't Go," "T-Model Blues" and "Tim Moore's Farm."

Hopkins spent the next ten or so years recording for several record companies—sometimes the same songs for different companies—and maintaining his local performance schedule. He refused to adapt his style in the 1950s as "blues turned toward the electric, band-based" recording style of "artists like Muddy Waters, Howlin' Wolf and B.B. King." Not only did he not want to change his sound, but Hopkins did not like to travel or adhere to record contracts, preferring to be paid in cash upon services rendered. Because of these attitudes, Hopkins's career plateaued for much of the 1950s.[98] His career peaked again in the 1960s with new interests in "authentic" blues from white blues and folk collectors who wanted more recordings from Lightnin'.[99] Hopkins spent the last twenty years of his life recording more of his own songs, performing across the world to integrated audiences with other blues artists and sharing the stage with rock bands that adored him and maintaining his home on Dowling Street. Throughout his career, he recorded about one hundred albums and six hundred to eight

Sam "Lightnin'" Hopkins in the studio. *Texas Music Collection, Special Collections, University of Houston Libraries.*

hundred songs. Twenty-plus years after his death, he was honored with a statue in Crockett, Texas (2002), and a historical marker by the City of Houston (2011) and received a Lifetime Achievement Grammy from the Recording Academy (2013).[100]

Beyond Lightnin' Hopkins, Houston also earned its spot on the map for blues-based music because of the hard work of Don Robey and Evelyn Johnson through their music companies: Duke Records, Peacock Records, Back Beat Records, Song Bird Records and the Buffalo Booking Agency. Although Robey is the person most commonly associated with these companies, as he was the owner, financier, negotiator and face, the success of these Houston-based music enterprises never would have happened without Johnson, who acted as the brains, manager and coordinator. Robey and Johnson were "responsible for a voluminous quantity of R&B, blues and gospel that was the foundation of one of the first, if not the first, music businesses run by a black man in this country."[101] Robey was born in Houston in 1903. He was the son of a Jewish man and a black woman. He grew up in Houston's historic Fifth Ward, which was his lifelong home and base for his businesses. His vocations prior to the music business included gambler, hustler, proprietor of a taxi business and club owner. Robey owned the Bronze Peacock Diner (a nightclub) in Houston's Fifth Ward. Johnson was a native south Louisianan who moved to Houston as a child with her family. After graduating from Phillis Wheatley, she worked as an X-ray technician at Houston's Memorial Hospital. Johnson left the hospital after becoming severely ill due to the dangerous working conditions, and she then managed and kept the books at the Bronze Peacock.[102] Her foray into the music business with Robey is said to have begun by chance, as the legend goes:

> One night [in 1947] at the Bronze Peacock, a young guitarist named Clarence "Gatemouth" Brown sat in for an ailing T-Bone Walker. Robey recognized a singular talent and started the Buffalo Booking Company so he could manage the young performer. He landed Brown a deal with a West Coast label, but when it produced no hits, he started his own Peacock Records label in 1949.[103]

Robey did not like the deal that he made with Aladdin Records, which gave him measly royalties and limited options. At the end of Brown's contract, Robey and Johnson found themselves in a prickly perch, "having a burgeoning blues star who now had no record company to popularize his work." Thus, Robey decided that he would put out his own records, assigning

Business card of Don D. Robey, owner of Duke-Peacock Records. *Texas Music Collection, Special Collections, University of Houston Libraries.*

Business card of Evelyn Johnson, owner of Buffalo Booking Agency. *Texas Music Collection, Special Collections, University of Houston Libraries.*

Johnson the task of figuring out the logistics for how to do so.[104] Christine M. Kreiser asserted that "Robey and the fledgling Peacock had moderate chart success with Brown and a handful of other artists, and he eventually closed the dinner club to concentrate on the music business. This move paid off in 1953, when Big Mama Thornton's Peacock single 'Hound Dog' went to

Clarence "Gatemouth" Brown. *Texas Music Collection, Special Collections, University of Houston Libraries.*

the top of the R&B charts."[105] Thornton, a Montgomery, Alabama native, made Houston her home for a period during the late 1940s into the 1950s. Thornton came to Houston in 1948 in hopes of transitioning from gospel recording to blues. She was the first recorder/performer of Jerry Leiber and Mike Stoller's song "Hound Dog," which held the number-one spot on the Billboard R&B charts for seven weeks in 1953.

In 1952, Robey entered into a partnership with David Mattis, founder and owner of the Memphis-based label Duke Records, and within the year, he took ownership. Andrew Dansby noted that this "deal [helped propel the success of Peacock Records because it] netted him some of Duke's key artists like Bobby "Blue" Bland, Junior Parker, and Johnny Ace."[106] Robey and Johnson would go on to manage the careers and successes of several blues, R&B and gospel artists out of their Fifth Ward entertainment companies. Their contributions to American popular music are important because their successes and contributions came almost a decade prior to the rise of Barry Gordy and Motown. Under the direction of Robey and Johnson, the following persons were among the many who garnered national

Johnny Ace. *Texas Music Collection, Special Collections, University of Houston Libraries.*

Bobby "Blue" Bland. *Texas Music Collection, Special Collections, University of Houston Libraries.*

The Dixie Hummingbirds. *Texas Music Collection, Special Collections, University of Houston Libraries.*

success: Clarence "Gatemouth" Brown, Marie Adams, Floyd Dixon, Big Mama Thornton, Johnny Ace, Junior Parker, Bobby "Blue" Bland, Mighty Clouds of Joy, The Dixie Hummingbirds, Five Blind Boys of Mississippi and many other musicians who backed national artists. These sidemen included "musicians, songwriters, singers, and arrangers such as Joe Scott, Pluma Davis, Clarence Hollimon, Teddy Reynolds, Hamp Simmons, Grady Gaines, Roy Gaines, Texas Johnny Brown, Calvin Owens, Pete Mayes, Lavelle White, Luvenia Lewis, Clarence Green, Joe Medwick [Masters], Joe Hughes, Oscar Perry" and many others.[107] In an interview with Wood,

Five Blind Boys of Mississippi. *Texas Music Collection, Special Collections, University of Houston Libraries.*

local bluesman Wilbur McFarland evinced, "You've got more historical musicians in Houston than, I believe, in any other city in the union. Because the blues artists that was real big back in the fifties and sixties—listen at me real good—T-Bone Walker, Lightnin' Hopkins, Amos Milburn, B.B. King, Bobby Bland, Gatemouth Brown, Junior Parker, Albert Collins…many of the musicians in town played with those artists."[108]

ZYDECO

Most people who have spent any time partying or vacationing in southwest Louisiana (New Orleans, Lake Charles, Lafayette or Baton Rouge) have probably two-stepped to the syncopated acoustic sounds of a fast-tempo accordion, a washboard, a double kick drum, an electric guitar and an indecipherable Creole-singing man or woman. That music form is called zydeco, and though it is most commonly associated with the cities and towns in southern and southwest Louisiana, its popularization and modernization can be attributed to Houston.

But zydeco is not just a music form; it is a culture. Zydeco culture hails from the small towns in rural southwest and southern Louisiana, where La Las or accordion dances were held to mollify the pains of a hard workweek. These dances also featured familiar music and good food, such as "gumbo, boudin, and folded pies." Most often, these dances were held in homes, and in many towns, they were held at Catholic churches as a fellowship activity.[109] This culture came to the Houston area with the black Creoles who left Louisiana for the "Beaumont area after oil spurted from Spindletop in 1901…[then more came as a result of] the floods of 1927…and the largest group came to Houston and East Texas after World War II in search of work."[110] Once in Houston, many of the migrants settled in the Fifth Ward in an area that in 1922 became known as Frenchtown. They merged their traditional folk-based acoustic music culture with the existing urbanized and electric black cultural forms in Houston, particularly the jazz and blues music played in popular clubs and juke joints. At this point, La La music morphed into zydeco. It was in Houston where its name and now-standard orthography was first used to describe the hybrid musical form, where it took on its modern form, where it was first recorded and where a few of its most important clubs were located.[111]

SOUL

As popular music tastes shifted, Houston artists jumped into the funk and soul music genres burgeoning in the 1960s and early 1970s. Skipper Lee Frazier, who was a disc jockey on KYOK and, later, KCOH, played a major role in taking Houston's soul/funk style to national audiences. Skipper managed and promoted many groups, but two groups "brought him and the city worldwide acclaim." The groups were Archie Bell and The Drells and the TSU Tornadoes. Their big hit was a very popular dance tune named "Tighten Up," "for which Frazier wrote the lyrics and the Tornadoes did the music."[112] Archie Bell and The Drells began "Tighten Up" by announcing to the world that they were from Houston, Texas:

Hi everybody, I'm Archie Bell of the Drells From Houston, Texas
We don't only sing but we dance just as good as we want

In Houston, we just started a new dance called the Tighten Up
This is the music we tighten up with.[113]

Michael Corcoran claimed, "The spoken intro was inspired by disparaging remarks made in the wake of the Kennedy assassination by a DJ who said nothing good came from Texas. [Bell recalled,] 'We were from Texas, and we were good, so we just let everybody know up front.'"[114] This was Archie's way of clarifying a misinterpretation of Houston.

As in other areas of the country, music production coming out of Houston, namely blues and R&B, declined in the 1970s. The primary reasons for this decline were corporate interest in homogenizing local/regional music, the club DJ and disco. Nelson George claimed in *The Death of Rhythm and Blues* (1988) that major record labels saw that black music could be sold to mass audiences and therefore bought up smaller labels like the ones owned and operated by Robey and began to package music like packaging bags of chips—making all of the music sound the same. Improvisation and creativity suffered in the face of corporate pressure to have a certain sound. Additionally, George argued that technology, specifically the mixer, changed the way people listened to music. The mixer allowed for continuous flow and play of music, which made music easier to dance to all night long. African American Houstonians fell in love with this dance music at the big clubs that began sprouting up around town. Those who did not get down with funk began to consume more jazz as a result of the jazz format featured on the college radio station, KTSU. Blues and soul music became more of an underground thing—left to working-class blacks and white fans—primarily played and performed at hole-in-the-wall clubs and venues.

These aforementioned artists and their original fans were among the African American Houstonians born before the civil rights movement, before the influx of crack in urban areas, before manufacturing facilities closed and before integration and suburbanization. The musicians and patrons of that generation were largely hopeful and worked hard to attain the American Dream within their segregated society. Their music generally expressed this hope, the travails of reaching the "dream" and the dancing that happened when they thought they had reached the "dream." And when their music did sing of despair, it wasn't raised to the level of "fuck it" or "fuck you." However, their kids, particularly those left in the ghettoes, would be exposed to a more ominous world that tended to push them to the margins. They were the answer to Langston Hughes's provocative question "What happens to a dream deferred?" This new generation was less hopeful, and their world was much more sinister. They were "left behind." They needed to tell their story, and they needed a new way to do so. With new technologies and grimy stories to tell, their way became known as hip-hop. It developed out of the Bronx and eventually made its way to Houston.

chapter 3

HIP-HOP TAKES ROOT IN HOUSTON

THE FORMATIVE STAGES OF HOUSTON'S HIP-HOP CULTURE (1979-86)

It was not long before similarly marginalized black and Hispanic communities in other cities picked up on the tenor and energy in New York hip-hop. Within a decade [of its public emergence], *Los Angeles County (especially Compton), Oakland, Detroit, Chicago, Houston, Atlanta, Miami, Newark and Trenton, Roxbury, and Philadelphia* [had] *developed local hip-hop scenes that link*[ed] *various regional postindustrial urban experiences of alienation, unemployment, police harassment, social, and economic isolation to their local and specific experience via hip-hop's language, style, and attitude. Regional differentiation in hip-hop has been solidifying and will continue to do so. In some cases, these differences are established by references to local streets and events, neighborhoods, and leisure activities. In other cases, regional difference can be discerned by their preference for dance steps, clothing, musical samples, and vocal accents. Like Chicago and Mississippi blues, these emerging regional identities of hip-hop affirm the specificity and local character of cultural forms, as well as the larger forces that define hip-hop and Afrodiasporic cultures. In every region, hip-hop articulates a sense of entitlement and takes pleasure in aggressive insubordination.*
—Tricia Rose, 1994[115]

In 1988, I did a piece for the Village Voice titled "Nationwide: America Raps Back" that argued, "Rap's gone national and is in the process of going regional. That seems like a contradiction, but actually its easily explained. Rap spread out from New York to attract a loyal national audience. Now America is rapping back." As evidence, I cited several factors: the founding of Rap-A-Lot Records in Houston, which would bring us the Geto Boys, and Luke Skywalker (soon to

*be Luke Records) in Miami, which would release the 2 Live Crew; the fact that
in a number of markets (Dallas, Houston, Cleveland, Detroit, Philadelphia,
Miami, Los Angles), certain rap records would sell more there than in New York
City, suggesting regional tastes were developing; and the local support systems
for rap that were springing up across the country, from Houston's huge rap clubs,
Rhinestone's and Spud's, to progressive rap programmers such as Lynn Tolliver in
Cleveland, who aggressively mixed rap with traditional R&B.*
—*Nelson George*[116]

Hip-hop arrived in Houston as the city began its transition from boom to bust. Sociologist Robert D. Bullard argued that Houston experienced a population boom in the mid-1970s due to vast economic and residential opportunities.[117] Yet in this same time of boom, economic and residential opportunities for blacks were slow to increase. Houston also began to experience mass suburbanization, which allowed middle-class blacks to escape segregated communities, leaving behind the working and poor classes. This flight, coupled with high unemployment, low-wage jobs and deteriorating public schools, made working-class black neighborhoods invisible and susceptible to increased criminal activity, surveillance and nihilism.

Unemployment rates for blacks in the early 1980s soared above that of whites, and blacks were more likely than whites to be employed in blue-collar positions.[118] In the early 1980s, Houston's economy began to falter due to its heavy concentration in the petrochemical industry, which experienced an oil glut and plunging prices.[119] As a result, Houston promoters began the "Houston Proud" campaign to defend the city against hard economic times. However, Houston could not be proud of the "depression-like" conditions in its older and segregated black neighborhoods.[120]

Despite these conditions of squalor, African Americans in Houston—poor, working and middle class—still found time for leisure and entertainment. A large segment of African Americans in Houston enjoyed soul, funk and R&B music in the late 1970s and early 1980s. Houston DJ, emcee and hip-hop personality Wicked Cricket, who split time between New York and Houston between the late 1960s and 1970s, recalled, "When I first got to Houston [in the late 1970s], bands played in clubs, [people wore] straight legs and red ropers, and the DJs didn't mix…they [would] tell you to scream, and when you screamed, they switched the record."[121] But in 1979–80, those Houstonians and their children were introduced to hip-hop music.

In a 2008 article for the *Houston Press*, writer Lance Scott Walker sought to find the origins of the city's hip-hop culture. He noted that "to pinpoint the birth of rap music in Houston is to place a number of pins along a scattered timeline of the late '70s and early '80s."[122] In the introduction of the article, he identified events that could signify the starting point of Houston's hip-hop culture. Although he mentioned several events (e.g. DJ Darryl Scott's mixtapes; Houston's first rap single, "MacGregor Park"; and the founding of Rap-A-Lot Records), Walker was unable to unequivocally proclaim an official start date of Houston's hip-hop culture.

But that theoretical date is not important in understanding how Houston began to participate in and appropriate hip-hop culture. What is important, as Walker noted, is determining those factors such as the persons, events and social contexts between 1979 and 1986 that led to the initial professionalization of Houston's hip-hop culture and contributed to its establishment as a hip-hop city. People like James Smith, Russell Washington and Troy Birklett—all Houston record-company owners who began in the late 1980s—did not just wake up one day and decide to begin record labels; there was a culture budding around them that they decided to professionalize and commodify.[123]

This budding culture consisted of young people imitating hip-hop culture that they were exposed to via radio and television, and it also consisted of Houston's systems of support: large clubs, a college radio station that broke new music and a large consumer base.

The disc jockey had held the prominent position in hip-hop culture since its development, but by the early 1980s, the rapper was beginning to take center stage. Although break dancing began to take the nation by storm in the early 1980s, the young people in Houston's ghettoes primarily stuck to the music. Carlos Garza (DJ Styles) recalled that there were a few break-dancing crews and competitions, but on the whole, Houstonians' early participation in the culture was through rapping and DJing.[124]

Even though the young African Americans who began rapping had other hobbies and extracurricular activities, rapping was something new and catchy that became part of their youth experience. It did not require any membership fees or uniforms; rapping required only that you had (or thought that you had) verbal dexterity. And these young dilettantes joined in, with no clue what might happen. DJ and radio personality Luscious Ice pointed out:

> [Hip-hop] *didn't cost any money—you didn't have to go with the Prince or Michael Jackson look…go to the mall and buy a $300 leather jacket with a bunch of zippers or go get an $80 or $90 jheri curl or look like Prince. These were real ghetto kids…everyday kids. Back in the day, the pretty-boy thing was very prevalent when R&B was going through its*

synthesizer phase…but with hip-hop, my next-door neighbor, who really did not have much, he could…actually imitate the hip-hop look. You didn't have to spend any money. It became economically feasible.[125]

Most young people who would become professional rappers got their start in schoolyards, project courtyards or on street corners in Houston's wards. Their raps were unsophisticated and usually took the form of "cap rapping" or narcissistic boasting.[126] Yet these were the initial opportunities for the budding rappers to earn their stripes and prove their lyrical skills before other opportunities arose. And just like hip-hop did not start off as a career move, these young people did not think that they would rap professionally; they were just attempting to mimic a new cultural expression and announce their existence to the world.[127]

Keith Rogers (Sire Jukebox) of Houston's Third Ward began as a beatboxer with his crew The Awesome 3 and Jukebox. He remembered that the content of his early battle raps was very elementary: "[It was like] 'I'm big, I'm bad, I'm this, I'm that!' It wasn't as flashy. It was more metaphors, similes and wordplays. There was a little storytelling in there."[128] Jukebox and his crew soon began battle rapping at Jack Yates High School and later performing at talent shows.[129] Once they gained more experience and confidence, they took their show on the road and battled kids from other neighborhoods and schools.

Eric Kaiser (K-Rino) first began rapping in 1983 while a student at Albert Thomas Middle School in Houston's South Park. The youngsters battle rapped and freestyled at every free moment.[130] Kaiser recalled, "You would walk up to a circle, and cats would be battling and freestyling." One day, when a "couple of [his] buddies…were battling, [he] wrote a rhyme for one of [his] friends…and [the friend] won with the rhyme." Kaiser thought to himself, "I could've done that myself!"[131] This inspired him to take rap seriously. He, too, began to battle rap, later forming the group Real Chill with two friends, Timothy Hood (G.T.) and James Conner (Preppy Jay). K-Rino's Real Chill became one of the first groups in Houston to record an album.

Willie Dennis's (Willie D) foray into rapping was also by happenstance. Willie began writing songs at the age of ten or eleven while living in Coke Apartments in the Fifth Ward. He used writing as a form of therapy in the face of his dark social and familial realities. He wrote R&B songs and performed his songs in talent shows. Though writing or performing raps was not something that he planned to do, one day, one of his close friends volunteered him for a rap challenge. He recalled:

K-Rino, circa 1980s. *Houston Hip-Hop Collection, Special Collections, University of Houston Libraries.*

I was in da hood in Fifth Ward. We used to hang out in da hood and sing old doo-wop—you know how they used to do the old doo-wop back in da day. We would sing whatever the current R&B song was of the day. We would be in the neighborhood just singing whenever we wasn't fighting. One day, we was hanging out, and somebody had the radio on and we was listenin' to Run-D.M.C.'s "Sucker MCs," and Steve, one of my buddies, was like, "Man, me and Willie can do that!" So I'm listenin' to it [and thinking], "Well, the rhyme scheme don't sound complex; it sound educated, but it don't sound complex." So Steve was like, "We gonna go in the house and come back out in one hour, and we gonna come back with our own stuff!" We came back in an hour, and I had like eight bars. He said his rap, and everybody started laughing, but when I said my rap, they started raising their eyebrows. They seemed impressed. So when I saw that...I started [thinking], "Maybe I got something right here!" That's how it all started—turning that lil' eight bars into a verse and eventually into a song.[132]

Once Willie transitioned to high school, he and another soon-to-be rapper, Romeo Poet, battled each other at Forest Brook on Houston's northeast side.

These rappers, in their embryonic stages, began to skip school to rap. They took the Houston Metro to other schools and battled other young rappers who had made a reputation for themselves. They had to show off their skills and claim more territory in their rapping conquests. K-Rino recalled:

We used to battle on street corners. Jukebox and Raheem used to come to Ross Sterling [High School] to battle me. That's what we used to do—we weren't thinking about making no records...we was warriors back then man. If we seen somebody who looked like they could rap, we was finna' battle. You bet' not wear no Kangol, no warm-up, none of that, cause we was gonna battle![133]

In 1980, Oscar Ceres (Raheem) moved to Missouri City, a Houston suburb, with his family from Trenton, New Jersey. To Oscar's chagrin, his mother and stepfather decided to move for better economic opportunities. Oscar wanted to stay in New Jersey so that he could still participate in its growing hip-hop culture. Raheem boasted, "I came to Houston with [hip-hop] in my blood...I was looking for people who were doing what I was doing. I tried to break-dance, but I wasn't really good at that—them boys was killing me. But I could piece those words together and rock a crowd."[134] He, too, found himself more intrigued with rapping than school, so he began to skip school to battle others. Oscar recalled that he met Jukebox in a quest to battle Prince Ezzy-E (Eric Woods, Original E of O.G. Style):

I was skipping school, and…the late, great, rest his soul Prince Ezzy-E at the time (later on, he became [Original E of] O.G. Style) had a tape that they played on Kidz Jamm, and I heard it and liked it. I was like, "Yo, that boy is nice!" And it was like, "Yo, I gotta battle him!" You see, back in those days, what a lot of people don't understand is that battling wasn't necessarily a bad thing: it was just your way of making your name in the hip-hop community. You had to show that you were worthy of being an emcee in the circle that was going on. When I heard the tape, I said, "I gotta find out who this dude is." And a lot of the cats from Missouri City that were into rap but did not rap themselves was like, "Yo, he go to Jack Yates!" I went to Jack Yates, so I was going with the intention of just battling him. And a battle back in those days was just a guy beating on the table or the door or somebody beatboxing and you spittin' your rhyme. So, I finally found out where he was. I was like starstruck because he had a tape playing on KTSU. We battled, and I guess they called it a draw or whatever, but from that point forward, it was like, "Okay, you accepted as a part of the click to a certain extent!" I met Jukebox, and Box was like, "You alright, you hot!" He gave me his number, and that's how me an him became friends—from me going to war, so to speak, with E.[135]

For those young people who could not rap but still wanted to be a part of the culture, they got acquainted with the "wheels of steel"—turntables. They would eventually become local DJs, radio personalities and music producers.

William Ross (Def Jam Blaster) moved with his family from the Fifth Ward to the Houston-incorporated city of Missouri City. He tried all of the elements of hip-hop culture but settled comfortably into DJing. His father had a huge music collection, and Ross was inspired by the way that DJs could scratch. Though he never aspired to be a party DJ, he did have a large record collection, which prompted his schoolmates and neighborhood friends to ask him to provide party tunes.[136]

Blaster had a friend with family connections on the East Coast who kept him informed about the latest DJ technology. When Blaster learned that DJs on the East Coast were beginning to use the cross fader to seamlessly segue from song to song, he "had to get one."[137] Soon, he hooked up with classmate Brad Jordan (DJ Akshen), a DJ and beatboxer, to start making music. DJ Akshen, who later took on the name Scarface, mentioned that he rapped as well. They then began to meet in the garage of another classmate, Marcus Wiley, to record songs. Wiley would go on to become a comedian, radio personality and college professor.

Anthony Harris (DJ Luscious Ice), from Houston's north side, was influenced by the on-air personalities/DJs from his favorite program, Kidz Jamm. Each week, he anxiously anticipated Saturday, when he could "hear Kidz Jamm…because [he] always heard [new music played by] Lester "Sir" Pace, Wicked Cricket and Jazzie Redd."[138] Although he was a track star in high school, he also had an affinity for music, especially this new form called hip-hop. He began to imitate the on-air personalities/DJs from Kidz Jamm and soon began a new extracurricular activity—DJing.

Luscious Ice began to DJ in 1984. He and fellow track team member Alan Jackson DJed a party for one of the black student organizations at their high school, Waltrip High, with two mismatched turntables and a Wellington mixer without pitch control. They failed to put fans on their amps; therefore, the amps blew out. Guests of the party left because there was no music. As a result, their cut—after the host and the security guard got theirs—was just fifteen dollars. He recalled:

> One of my homeboys from Chicago was with us. I remember him busting out laughing 'cause we only got fifteen dollars to DJ this party. But we learned about equipment and quality control…doing parties and that type of thing, which was a growing process. That was in '84. That was one of those situations where your library of records was the records in your mama's house and maybe a couple of hit records that was out at the time— but that was your library. I remember one time we played "Let's Go Crazy" by Prince five times at the same party. We only had about ten records that were current records, so we played records over and over again. That is what propelled me to want to do it. I loved the [hip-hop] music.[139]

The aforementioned rappers, DJs and other unmentioned Houston hip-hoppers would soon cross paths and join forces through Houston's systems of support—those places that allowed hip-hop to grow in Houston and those places that showcased Houston's hip-hop talent.

Nelson George noted in his 1988 *Village Voice* article that record industry types used to ask him, "How long will this rap thing last?" When it arrived on the public scene in the early 1980s, many people thought it was only a passing fad. But as George explained, "Rap and its hip-hop musical underpinning" had gone national and was then the new "national youth music of black America and the dominant dance music of urban America."[140] As evidence for his claims, George listed the new start-up labels and groups across the country and those local systems of support that buttressed the culture. He also noted that "in each city where rap's appeal [had] expanded, there [were] key figures [who] fought authorities, peer pressure, and local inferiority complexes" to ensure that hip-hop had a place.[141] He pointed to Houston as an example. He singled out the city because of the valiant efforts of Steve Fournier—DJ, club promoter, owner of a large record pool and, later, a regional rep for Def Jam Records—and because of Houston's large and bustling hip-hop nightclubs. What George failed to mention in his article was that Houston was also becoming a hip-hop city because of a local college radio station and its large consumer base. Hip-hop flourished in Houston so much that, according to Steve Fournier, George, Russell Simmons, Lyor Cohen and others began to pay attention and visit the city. By 1991, Houston had become the second-largest consumer market of hip-hop music and hip-hop concerts in the country.[142]

HOUSTON'S LARGE NIGHTCLUBS: FROM RAY BARNETT TO THE RHINESTONE WRANGLER

Black nightclubs in Houston have been around since blacks first settled in their segregated wards. Some were small juke joints, while others were larger venues where local and national bands entertained local blacks and whites alike. Houston's nightclub history included places like the Bronze Peacock Diner, Shady's Playhouse, Club Matinee, the Eldorado Ballroom, Club Ebony and many more. By the late 1960s, one man controlled a critical mass of the Houston nightclub scene for African Americans—Ray Barnett.

Barnett was born in Opelousas, Louisiana, in 1931. His family later moved to Houston's Fifth Ward, where Barnett graduated from Phillis Wheatley High School. After serving in the army and attending Cornell University, Barnett returned to Houston and began a successful career in the entertainment business. He was so successful, in fact, that he became known as the "Godfather of Nightclubs" because he owned so many popular clubs and mentored many others who would become club owners or promoters. Houston club promoter Guy Bouldin recalled:

If you were a [black] young adult in Houston in the '60s, you had two choices: you could either wait until you graduated college and got married before you could have a drink in public or you could join a club and have a mixed drink, even if you were underage. Ray Barnett had a nightclub in

Houston called The Xcalibur. You could dance, but you couldn't buy drinks in there because it was BYOB. The astute nightclub mogul opened a private club inside the Xcalibur called the Xke Club, and it was strictly private membership only and therefore avoided the liquor-by-the-drink restrictions. Ray Barnett's conglomerate of clubs also included the Cinder Club on Dixie Drive, the Casino Royale on Almeda, the Latin World off Harrisburg and The Sands of Houston during the '60s. Way before black athletes were getting multi-million-dollar contracts and rappers started using the word "bling," Mr. Barnett was living larger than life.[143]

Singer Trudy Lynn made a special mention of Barnett in the book *Texas Blues: The Rise of a Contemporary Sound* (2008) because she felt that much of the discourse about entertainment history in Houston downplayed or even omitted his contributions. Lynn noted that she first saw Redd Foxx, Etta James and many other R&B greats at one of Barnett's clubs and that being at his Cinder Club was like "being on top."[144] Barnett's influence on black club-goers continued throughout the last third of the twentieth century, but in the early 1980s, his hold on the black market was usurped by new clubs that catered to a crowd of young adults who eschewed pomp and circumstance in exchange for loud music, DJs' scratching and casual clothes. This was the hip-hop generation, and their Ray Barnett was a man by the name of Steve Fournier.

Steve Fournier, circa 1980s. *Courtesy of Steve Fournier.*

Steve Fournier did not look like your typical hip-hopper. Fournier was a "stocky, bearded white guy" who fell in love with "black" music as a child living on the south side of Chicago. He later developed a lifelong romance with hip-hop culture and its music.[145] In 1965, when Fournier was nine years old, his widowed mother married an electrician from Kinder, Louisiana, and at the end of the race riots of 1965, his stepfather got a job with a Texas oil company and moved the family to Houston. They settled in a home on the northeast side of town, off of Lakewood Drive and Mesa Road, which at the time was a mixed-race community. Fournier attended M.B. Smiley High School, and while a student, his parents' teaching on race neutrality was met head on with prominent racial divisions—white kids hung in their cliques, and black kids in their cliques. Fournier felt like an outsider because he liked all people. In his senior year, this amiability was challenged, and he met a conflict that served as a defining moment and set a precedent for how he would handle all those who tried to force him into racial and musical polarities. Fournier recalled:

> *A turning point…came when I was* [driving around with] *two or three kids in the car…I pushed the button* [to turn the radio station], *and when the music started playing, they go, "You listen to that music?" The people in the car…all of them were my friends for the last couple of years.*
>
> *I go, "What do you mean 'that music?'" They go, "That's black music."*
>
> *Me, being naïve and raised as I was…looked at the radio thinking, "No, it's orange." You know I thought they meant the radio station was black or the thing had turned black. So I said, "What do you mean?"*
>
> *"Well, that's black music—we don't listen to black music."*
>
> *I asked, "You mean the song?"*
>
> *"Yeah."*
>
> *"Are y'all crazy or what? I love this music."*
>
> *At that point…I said, "Whoa!" I never knew there was a difference; I always just thought music was music. I looked at those kids, and I stopped my car and told them to all leave. I said, "Get out of my car! If y'all are this racist, I can't even believe you are my friends." I never talked to them again. I never seen them again since that day. All these years and years ago…that's how I stuck to my guns. I said, "I love this music."*[146]

After graduation, Fournier got married and then began to hang out in Houston nightclubs. Since the music that he loved was called "black music," he frequented the black nightclubs where it was played. Fournier's main job between 1976 and 1979 was as a "club head," as he bounced around nightspots to hear the likes of Parliament-Funkadelic, Sly and the Family Stone, The Bar-Kays, Con Funk Shun and other funk music.[147] While hanging out at all those clubs, Fournier fell in love with the mechanics of the DJ who spun at The Park club on Aldine Mail Route Road. He recalled that he'd "just hang around the DJ booth thinking 'Ah, this is great, this guy

[is] surrounded by girls!'"[148] Eventually, the DJ came to recognize him. One night, the DJ asked Fournier to watch his turntables while he took a restroom break. This became a regular routine. Fournier recalled that he "would wait all night until [the DJ] had to use the restroom just so [he] could watch those turn tables [and get his chance to stand in the] DJ booth."[149] One night, the DJ fell ill, so the club owners allowed Fournier to DJ for about thirty minutes—with a drink for his payment. He soon learned the basics of DJing and caught the attention of an eager entrepreneur. Fournier recollected that in 1979, a white gentleman approached him and said, "I'm opening a club, and it's gonna be the biggest black club ever in the city of Houston and I want you to DJ—will you do it?'" Fournier "didn't even ask him how much he was gonna [be paid]." With the blessing of the DJ that trained him, he immediately agreed to the job and went on to be the DJ at Struts Disco.[150]

Struts was an anomaly to black clubs because instead of packing 200 to 300 people in the club on one night like Ray Barnett and Charles Bush were able to do in their clubs, Struts "was packed every single night" with up to 1,300 people. The clubs that Barnett and Bush owned and managed were primarily located on the south side of Houston, with less space for parking and less square footage for dancing. At Struts, Fournier was able to mix in the music that he had recently fallen in love with—rap.[151]

Like other early hip-hop enthusiasts, Fournier was exposed to hip-hop via "Rapper's Delight" and a few of the other early songs coming out of New York—Jimmy Spicer's "Adventure of Super Rhymes" (1980), Grandmaster Flash and The Furious Five's "Superrappin'" (1979), Kurtis Blow's "Christmas Rappin'" (1980) and T/Ski Valley's "Catch a Beat" (1981). The owner did not understand why Fournier continuously slipped hip-hop into his mixes. Fournier again found himself defending his music tastes, and again he did not stand down. Instead of engaging in an argument, Fournier demonstrated what happened when he played the R&B music compared to when he played rap songs. The dance floor was sparse when R&B and pop songs were played but was fully packed when hip-hop was played. As long as the people stayed on the dance floor, they worked up a sweat and then ran to the bar for drinks. Seeing this was enough for the owner to back down.[152]

Within two years, Struts peaked. The owner decided he had made enough money, and in 1981, he decided to close the club. Knowing this, another eager entrepreneur approached Fournier, saying, "I understand they are about to close Struts…I'm gonna open a club bigger than [Struts]." Fournier could not believe that there could be something bigger than Struts, but the entrepreneur said, "I have this country western club [that] I'm gonna flip, and I'm gonna call it Boneshaker's."[153]

Boneshaker's was located on Houston's north side off of Interstate 45 and Aldine Bender and was a turning point in Houston's hip-hop culture. With Fournier as the DJ and promoter, more and more hip-hop music was played. Couple that with the fact that the club was filled to capacity—over one thousand patrons—each night, and more people in Houston were exposed to the latest hip-hop sounds. Fournier even maneuvered his way into booking Kurtis Blow and the World Class Wrecking Crew in Houston to perform at Boneshaker's. Regional representatives from hip-hop record labels were amazed by the large crowds of people jamming and consuming their music. Fournier noted that these representatives went back to New York to brag about the club phenomenon in Houston.

During the four years that Boneshaker's was open, Fournier began to travel to New York to develop relationships with DJs and record companies so that he could get more of the music that he wanted to play in his club. One influential relationship that he developed was with hip-hop pioneer DJ Red Alert. Red Alert and record label representatives sent Fournier albums in the mail so that he could break new music in Houston. At this time, Houston radio stations—KCOH, KYOK, Love 94 and Majic 102—played hip-hop music sporadically, but Fournier claimed that the radio personalities and DJs would often come to him to get extra copies of the hot stuff. To get more play on the radio, he used rap music as the backing tracks for his club advertisements,

Name badge for the 1988 South by Southwest Music and Media Conference. *Courtesy of Steve Fournier.*

Above: Name badge for the 1991 South by Southwest Music and Media Conference. *Courtesy of Steve Fournier.*

Left: Name badge for the 1987 New Music Seminar. *Courtesy of Steve Fournier.*

Name badge for the 1988 New Music Seminar. *Courtesy of Steve Fournier.*

which enticed customers and spread the culture. People traveled from all over the region to party at Boneshaker's, and the club became so popular that the owner opened another location in Alexandria, Louisiana, where he had a home. Fournier and the owner traveled back and forth between Houston and Alexandria to maintain the business. Like Struts, Boneshaker's ran its course and was set to be closed. But before Boneshaker's actually shut its doors, Fournier was approached by a third eager entrepreneur with an offer to be the DJ for a new club called the Rhinestone Wrangler.

The Rhinestone Wrangler was located on South Main near the Houston Astrodome and is the place that many people remember most because of its diverse signature events. Keith Rogers (Sire Jukebox) claimed, "Hip-hop in Houston really caught on with the battle rapping at the Rhinestone Wrangler."[154] Nelson George described the Rhinestone Wrangler as a "big barn of a dancehall…and because of its '110 percent rap' policy, the place became the Gilley's of hip-hop."[155] The club owner gave Fournier total autonomy over the playlists; all the owner wanted was for thousands of people to pack the club. Young people flocked to the Rhinestone Wrangler to learn the latest dance moves, jam to the latest hip-hop songs and play witness to the battle-rap contests.

Every Sunday night, Fournier hosted the Rap Connection—a two-part rapping contest that pit rappers against each other to see who had the best lyrical skills. The Rap Connection showcased Houston's best rappers, which included Romeo Poet, Thelton Polk (K9/Sir-Rap-A-Lot), Willie D, Ricardo Royal, Jukebox, Class C, K-Rino and others. The contest also attracted the attention of out-of-town MCs who wanted to test their skills. One such out-of-town contestant was Robert Matthew Van Winkle (Vanilla Ice), a white guy from a Dallas suburb who would later sell millions of records with his song "Ice Ice Baby."[156] Winners received cash prizes and, more importantly, notoriety. In the first round, rappers battled each other, rapping over any instrumental they found. The second part of the contest was a ranking/cap-rapping contest in which rappers "could cut down other rappers."[157] Willie D became one of the best cap rappers in the city. He recalled, "I used to kick ass every Sunday…the last thirteen weeks in a row that the club was open, I won all thirteen."[158] DJ Ready Red corroborated this claim, noting that Willie was so good that he "was given the title 'Rankmaster.'"[159]

Stetsasonic at the Ultimate Rhinestone Wrangler, 1988. *Courtesy of Carlos Garza (DJ Styles).*

The Rhinestone Wrangler was also the official location for a few of Houston's rising DJs, notably R.P. Cola, who also mentored "Chris Martin, the kid who'd become DJ Premier, one of New York hip-hop's most influential producers of the '90s."[160] R.P. Cola and other DJs kept the Rhinestone Wrangler packed every night, playing the latest music coming out during the "Golden Age of Hip-Hop" (1984–92), including Run-D.M.C., Too Short, Eric B. & Rakim, Public Enemy, Stetsasonic, Beastie Boys, 2 Live Crew and many others.[161]

Fournier claimed that the Rhinestone Wrangler was so popular that it caught the attention of Russell Simmons and Lyor Cohen from Def Jam Records in New York. According to Fournier, they wanted to understand how a Houston nightclub was so popular and productive. Fournier related that Nelson George was sent to Houston by Simmons to report on the success of Houston's systems of support. The Rhinestone Wrangler also attracted the attention of local entrepreneur James Smith, who would soon professionalize the culture and have part ownership in the second installment of the club, the Ultimate Rhinestone Wrangler, located on the north side of Houston.

The Rhinestone Wrangler was not the only club that grew hip-hop's popularity in Houston—other clubs included Flashes, Gucci, The Rock, Palladium, Buffalo Soldiers, Cartoons and Spud's. For those too young to attend these clubs, skating rinks such as Fondren Great Skate, Rainbow Roller Rink, Super Skate and Lockwood Skating Rink offered opportunities to hear and dance to hip-hop music. DJs such as DJ Wicked Cricket, Captain Jack, Walter D and Lonnie Mack were a few of the men behind the wheels of steel that kept the parties going at Houston nightclubs and skating rinks. Although the club culture in Houston

Heavy D & the Boyz at Rainbow Roller Rink, 1987. *Courtesy of Carlos Garza (DJ Styles).*

79

Carlos "DJ Styles" Garza at the Ultimate Rhinestone Wrangler, 1990. *Courtesy of Carlos Garza (DJ Styles).*

THE RHINESTONE RANGLER
PRESENTS

LIVE AND IN CONCERT
It's
BOBBY JIMMY
& THE CRITTERS

GOOD
FOR ONE
ADMISSION

FRIDAY
OCT. 28
1988

Doors
Open at
8:00

THE
RHINESTONE
RANGLER
I-45 North
478 Parker Rd.
Houston, Texas
(713) 691-5405

Pre-Sale - $6.50   At the Door - $8.00

HRAP1 GENADM GEN ADM   COMP   EHRAP1
EVENT CODE SECTION/AISLE ROW/BOX SEAT ADMISSION EVENT CODE
.00 GENERAL ADMIT.   .00 GENERAL
ADMIT.
GENADM   SEC GENADM
SECTION/AISLE
PP   1X   58311
GEN ADM   ROW GEN
ROW/BOX SEAT
QRH1646   .00
C185EPh   SEAT ADM

QUATRO PRDUCTIONS PRES.
FALL RAP FEST FEATURING
THE BOOGIE BOYS AND THE
L.A. DREAM TEAM
CARTOONS/3680 S. GESSNER
FRI SEP 26 1986 8:00 PM

THANK YOU FOR
SUPPORTING
THIS EVENT

ALL TAXES INCLUDED
NO REFUND
NO EXCHANGE

E213616

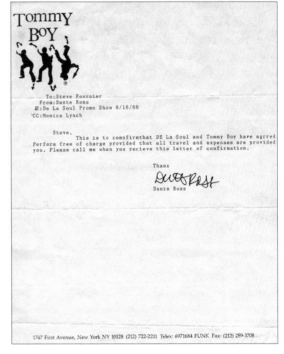

Top: Concert ticket for Eazy-E and NWA at the Ultimate Rhinestone Wrangler, 1988. *Courtesy of Steve Fournier.*

Middle: Concert ticket for Sir Mix-A-Lot and De La Soul, 1988. *Courtesy of Steve Fournier.*

Right: Performance confirmation letter from Tommy Boy Records for De La Soul performance at the Ultimate Rhinestone Wrangler, 1988. *Courtesy of Steve Fournier.*

Opposite, middle: Concert ticket for Bobby Jimmy and the Critters at the Ultimate Rhinestone Wrangler, 1988. *Courtesy of Steve Fournier.*

Opposite, bottom: Concert ticket for the Fall Rap Fest, featuring the Boogie Boys and the L.A. Dream Team, at Cartoons, 1986. *Courtesy of Steve Fournier.*

was a major system of support for hip-hop culture, it was not the only factor that helped Houston become a hip-hop city. There was also a local college radio station that featured the latest hip-hop music from across the country and gave many local artists their first radio play: Texas Southern's KTSU.

KIDZ JAMM:
DELIVERING HIP-HOP THROUGH THE AIRWAVES

Texas Southern University (TSU), located in the heart of Houston's Third Ward community, started KTSU's broadcast as a ten-watt FM radio station in 1972. Sometimes called the "Black Jewel," KTSU's programming centered primarily on jazz, blues and gospel for its first ten years in operation. In fact, its "Sunday Morning Gospel" program was the number-one-rated show in Houston for a number of years.

In 1981, KTSU general manager and one of Houston's first African-American broadcasters, Charles Porter, launched a weekly radio program for his high school–aged children, Stacy Porter and Charles Porter Jr. The plan was to teach the kids radio by allowing them to run and program a weekend show centered on youth music and culture. The show was called Kidz Jamm. This decision was made to the chagrin of Program Director Pam Collins, who did not want to babysit any high school kids or give up her weekends.

Contrary to the popular narrative, Kidz Jamm did not begin as a hip-hop program. The original team—Stacy Porter, Charles Porter Jr. and Michael Mitchell—played R&B and pop music, as hip-hop music was still not widely available. But that all changed in early 1982, when high school student Lester "Sir" Pace came to work for the show.

Pace spent his elementary school years in Houston's Third Ward. After his mother accepted a higher-paying job, his family moved to the northeast side of Houston near M.B. Smiley. At Smiley, Pace was an athlete and a member of the speech and debate teams, and he also read the morning announcements. When Pace first heard hip-hop music, he knew he had discovered a new hobby, and he began rapping and performing in talent shows with his friends Thelton Polk, Anthony Watson and Melvin Dewalt. Additionally, he worked at the McDonald's located on Little York Road at Highway 59, where he practiced his rapping skills while working the drive-through window. He would rap:

We got Big Macs, Quarter Pounders, french fries and apple pies
Chicken nuggets, chocolate shakes, scrambled eggs and hotcakes
What can I do for you today?[162]

During his junior year, one of Pace's teachers—a close friend of Pam Collins—suggested that he consider becoming a radio disc jockey. At first, he did not understand the job of a radio disc jockey, but he decided to follow her recommendation. Pace caught the Houston Metro to the KTSU studios every weekend to learn the fundamentals of radio. One day, he was left alone to do the show because the rest of the team was attending a game-day parade. Since the DJs had the leeway to play their own music, Pace began to slip in a few hip-hop albums. Pam Collins did not like this and called into the station that day, ordering him to stop. But Collins slowly became more comfortable with playing hip-hop on the station, especially after listeners began to demand it more than R&B. Pace claimed that one Saturday during the segment "Be Yourself"—a segment focused on teen social and political issues—the team conducted a call-in poll to determine what the listeners wanted to hear. Hip-hop won over R&B, thus initiating the transition of Kidz Jamm to a hip-hop format.

Pace's best friend was Walter Jones (Walter D), a young man who illegally hung around Boneshaker's and also DJed at a local skating rink, Super Skate. Whatever music Pace did not have, Walter had, so he either borrowed from Walter D or went downtown to buy his own records. As the popularity of Kidz Jamm rapidly increased, Pace caught the attention of DJ Polo Cool, who made Pace an offer to DJ at a rival skating rink, Rainbow. Soon, Pace drew larger crowds during his nights at Rainbow Skating Rink than Walter D was able to draw because Pace used Kidz Jamm to promote his gig.

Kidz Jamm aired every Saturday from 10:00 a.m. to 2:00 p.m., and the DJs on the show played the latest hip-hop from across the country. Kidz Jamm was also instrumental in breaking new music from local artists. If you were a local rap artist trying to get your music heard, Kidz Jamm was the place to take your tape. "Kidz Jamm was that one radio station where you could just walk in with your cassette tape, and as long as it was clean, they would play it right then," claimed K-Rino. "We would make a song, put it on tape and rush it to Kidz Jamm for Saturday."[163] Kidz Jamm was noted for breaking Scarface's first single, "Scarface"; Real Chill's first single; and many other local artists' first professional music offerings.[164]

To mitigate her concerns about babysitting the young people, Collins treated the Kidz Jamm volunteer staff like adults and taught them how to run a radio show. As such, it was a major training ground for many DJs, radio personalities, producers and even a few rappers. When Luscious Ice arrived at Texas Southern University in 1986 on a track scholarship, he got his first job as an intern on Kidz Jamm. Lester "Sir" Pace (now a record music executive), rapper Jazzie Redd, rapper and producer King Tee (Roger McBride, King T, Terry T), actress and radio personality Tammy McCall, New York radio personality Shelly Wade, Marcus Love, Parrish Murphy, Carvel J and Wicked Cricket all got their start at Kidz Jamm and went on to have success on the national level. Further, many of the popular local radio DJs of the 1990s began their careers with Kidz Jamm.

Kidz Jamm is significant for four reasons: (1) it was trailblazing, (2) it spread the music, (3) it broke talent and (4) it acted as a community outlet. Though Los Angeles radio station KDAY is often lauded and singled out as the first hip-hop radio station, Kidz Jamm, as a radio program, appeared at the same time and lasted longer. Along with the proliferation of new music in Houston's large nightclubs, Kidz Jamm was also responsible for breaking new hip-hop music, as it was the lone station in Houston playing it. Kidz Jamm assisted in the professionalization of Houston's hip-hop culture because it jump-started the careers of many early rappers. Kidz Jamm was instrumental in shaping Houston's hip-hop culture, as the show allowed for consistent participation in and access to hip-hop culture. When hip-hop acts came to Houston to perform, they stopped by Kidz Jamm to interact with their local fans.

SOUNDWAVES

As a result of Kidz Jamm and the large hip-hop clubs, a homegrown hip-hop market emerged in Houston. Houstonians wanted their own copies of the music they heard on the radio and in the clubs—the Bayou City was becoming a promising consumer market for hip-hop. However, few record shops in Houston carried hip-hop, and the shops that did had only the most popular records in stock. But in the late 1980s, the Houstonian hip-hip aficionado's demand was met with Soundwaves, located on South Main near the Rhinestone Wrangler and the Astrodome. The store became the leading record shop and carried much of the latest hip-hop.

In 1977, Bellaire High School graduate and University of Houston dropout surfer Jeff Spargo opened his first Soundwaves near Houston's

Hobby Airport. Soundwaves created a business model tailored to fit neighborhood demand. Spargo, who did not consider himself "a suburban guy and who hate[ed] country and folk [music]," stocked each store with the most popular music that his local customers partied to.[165] Hence, its second location on South Main stocked a lot of jazz, blues, R&B, funk, soul and old-school rock-and-roll for its urban customers. As hip-hop gained popularity in the mid-1980s, Soundwaves began to stock hip-hop albums in scattered amounts. But when Spargo's staff hired Carlos Garza in 1986, the hip-hop selection—and sales—soon increased.

Carlos Garza and his family migrated to Houston from Mexico in the late 1970s. They soon became resident aliens and moved to Houston's Third Ward. As a teenager at Bellaire, Garza fell in love with hip-hop culture after watching films like *Krush Groove* and *Breakin'*. Garza began break dancing and with a few of his friends created the Dynamic Crew. They competed in contests across the city in nightspots and parks. But after about one year, his break-dancing desires died down, and he transitioned to DJing, taking on the name DJ Styles. Garza was one of Soundwaves' best customers and would go to the store to get copies of the latest hip-hop that he heard on Kidz Jamm.

DJ Styles's first setup, 1984. *Courtesy of Carlos Garza (DJ Styles).*

DJ Styles's vinyl collection, mid-1980s. *Courtesy of Carlos Garza (DJ Styles).*

Patti Pantoja and Carlos "DJ Styles" Garza at Soundwaves. *Courtesy of Carlos Garza (DJ Styles).*

He spent so much time in the store that he eventually applied to work there after a suggestion from an employee. Shop owners Terry and Patti Pantoja hired DJ Styles and reaped great benefits.[166]

Styles immediately removed the hip-hop music out of the rock-and-roll section and created an entirely new section for hip-hop tapes and albums. When the management staff noticed his ingenuity, they made him responsible for ordering all of the hip-hop music, a job for which his DJing and devotion to Kidz Jamm made him well suited. During the course of his job, Styles developed relationships with the major hip-hop labels such as Tommy Boy, Def Jam Records, Tuff City and Wild Pitch Records. As a result, Soundwaves became the most exclusive record shop in Houston for hip-hop music. Club DJs and hip-hop fans from across Houston came to Styles' Soundwaves to satiate their taste for hip-hop music. Terry Hayes, who worked for Soundwaves competitor Wherehouse Music, remembered that her company "always battled with them because they'd get all the cool rap at their South Main store and drive us crazy."[167]

DJs also flocked to Soundwaves to purchase hard-to-find soul, jazz and funk music to use in their tracks. One such DJ was a college student by the name of Chris Martin. Martin, who then went by the DJ name Waxmaster C, was a student at Prairie View A&M University. His parents—father a university dean and mother a school librarian—had a huge music selection that Martin explored. He often traveled between Houston and Prairie View to DJ parties and stop by Soundwaves to pick up new hip-hop and dig for obscure jazz. One day, DJ Styles noticed Martin changing price stickers on the albums that he

Carlos Garza in Soundwaves, 1987. *Courtesy of Carlos Garza (DJ Styles).*

Big Daddy Kane (center) at Soundwaves, 1988. *Courtesy of Carlos Garza (DJ Styles).*

Big Daddy Kane signing albums at Soundwaves, 1988. Also in the picture is Patti Pantoja. *Courtesy of Carlos Garza (DJ Styles).*

DJ Jazzy Jeff and the Fresh Prince at Soundwaves, 1988. *Courtesy of Carlos Garza (DJ Styles).*

Fresh Fran, Original E and DJ Storm, 1988. *Courtesy of Carlos Garza (DJ Styles).*

Patti Pantoja, Naughty by Nature, Big Mello and DJ Styles at Soundwaves. *Courtesy of Carlos Garza (DJ Styles).*

DJ Premier, 1989. *Courtesy of Carlos Garza (DJ Styles).*

DJ Premier and DJ Storm at Soundwaves. *Courtesy of Carlos Garza (DJ Styles).*

wanted to purchase. When Martin arrived at the counter, Styles confronted him about his chicanery and then charged him the real price. Despite this confrontation, Styles and Martin soon developed a good friendship, and Martin also began working at Soundwaves. Styles remembered that he was taken away with the DJ skills of Martin, not only because of his seamless transitions and scratching but also because of the diversity of music that he used to keep people on the dance floor.[168]

Chris Martin also produced music for his group Inner Circle Posse (ICP), which consisted of friends from Prairie View A&M University. One day, he let Styles listen to ICP's demo tape. As soon as Styles heard the demo, he knew that he had to do something with it. By 1989, Styles had developed tight relationships with record labels in New York, so he contacted Stu Fine of Wild Pitch Records to sell him on the demo and encourage a meeting. Martin was already traveling back and forth between Houston and New York (staying with his grandfather while in New York), so it was easy for him to meet with Fine. Fine showed artist/A&R representative Keith Elam (Guru) the demo, and they both loved Martin's skills. Guru had a need for a new DJ for his group Gang Starr, so he brought on Martin, who soon changed his name to DJ Premier and began crafting the 1990s New York sound.[169]

Guru at Soundwaves. *Courtesy of Carlos Garza (DJ Styles).*

STEPHEN M.J. FOURNIER

OWNER / PRESIDENT
OF:

THE RAP POOL OF AMERICA
STEVE FOURNIER RAP PROMOTIONS
STEVE FOURNIER ENTERTAINMENT INC.

RAP POOL HOTLINE / RAP PROMOTIONS
PHONE: (713) 531-7970
FAX: (713) 531-8148
PAGER: (713) 746-6163

2379 BRIARWEST BLVD. #131   HOUSTON, TX 77077

Steve Fournier's business card. *Courtesy of Steve Fournier.*

At the same time that Soundwaves became a major source for hip-hop music, Steve Fournier began to take advantage of Houston's location to supply hip-hop music to DJs. In 1985, at the suggestion of Bill Stephney of Def Jam Records, Fournier founded the Rap Pool of America to distribute hip-hop

THE RAP POOL OF AMERICA
THE OFFICIAL RAP TOP 50

TOP 50 LIST   DATE: 10-1-90 TO 10-12-90

TC	LC	ARTIST	RAP TITLE	LABEL
1.	31	TOO SHORT	"THE GETTHO"	JIVE
2.	29	LL COOL J	"MAMA SAID KNOCK YOU OUT/LP"	DEF JAM
3.	13	D-NICE	"CALL ME D-NICE"	JIVE
4.	7	ICE CUBE	"ONCE UPON TIME IN THE PROJECTS"	PRIORITY
5.	23	KING TEE	"PLAYED YOU LIKE A PAINO"	CAPITOL
6.	24	ERIC B & RAKIM	"MAHOGANY"	MCA
7.	4	PUBLIC ENEMY	"I CAN'T DO NOTHIN FOR YA MAN"	DEF JAM
9.	5	POOR RIGHTEOUS TEACHERS	"ROCK THIS FUNKY JOINT"	PROFILE
9.	35	TRIBE CALLED QUEST	"BONITA APPELBUM"	JIVE
10.	3	K-SOLO	"YOUR MOM'S IN MY BUSINESS"	ATLANTIC
11.	40	X-CLAN	"FUNKIN LESSON"	ISLAND
12.	27	3RD BASS	"PRODUCTS OF THE ENVIRONMENT"	DEF JAM
13.	39	KOOL G RAP & DJ POLO	"STREETS OF NEW YORK"	COLD CHILLIN
14.	12	STETSASONIC	"SPEAKING OF A GIRL NAMED SUZIE"	TOMMY BOY
15.	8	KWAME	"OWNLESS EWE"	ATLANTIC
16.	2	YZ & G ROCK	"THE TOWER"	TUFF CITY
17.	-	THE JAZ	"ORIGINATORS"	EMI
18.	1	SIR-MIX-ALOT	"MY HOOPTIE"	NASTYMIX
19.	9	THE GETHO BOYS	"NO SELLOUT"	RAP-A-LOT
20.	28	GREGORY D & MANNY FRESH	"CLAP TO THIS"	YO RECORDS
21.	10	KBG	"THE BIG PAYBACK"	SELECT
22.	21	RHYTHM RADICALS	"BROTHER TO BROTHER"	LUKE RECORDS
23.	26	LOW PROFILE	"FUNKY SONG"	PRIORITY
24.	19	POISON CLAN	"THE GIRL THAT I HATE"	LUKE RECORDS
25.	30	PHASE & RHYTHM	"SWOLLEN POCKETS"	TOMMY BOY
26.	-	NWA	"100 MILES AND RUNNING"	PRIORITY
27.	17	RICH NICE	"OUTSTANDING"	MOTOWN
28.	20	THE D.O.C.	"LET THE BASS GO"	RUTHLESS
29.	16	DEF JEF	"BLACK TO THE FUTURE"	DELICIOUS VI.
30.	-	CHOICE	"THE BIG PAYBACK"	RAP-A-LOT
31.	-	FRESHCO AND MIZ	"AIN'T YOU FRESHCO"	TOMMY BOY
32.	11	CHILL ROB G	"THE POWER"	WILD PITCH
33.	25	SALT & PEPA	"INDEPENDENT WOMAN-REMIX"	NEXT PLATEAU
34.	14	NICE & SMOOTH	"FUNKY FOR YOU"	FRESH
35.	18	BIZZIE BOYZ	"DROPPIN IT"	YO RECORDS
36.	-	SPECIAL ED	"THE MISSION"	PROFILE
37.	-	ISIS	"FACE THE BASE"	4TH & BROAD
39.	43	BLVD. MOSSE	"YOU CAN'T ESCAPE THE HYPENESS"	SCORPIO
40.	49	VANILLA ICE	"ICE, ICE BABY"	SBK
41.	32	KID & PLAY	"BACK TO BASIX"	SELECT
42.	22	THE AFROS	"FEEL IT"	JMJ RECORDS
43.	-	NIKKI D	"LETTIN OFF STEAM"	DEF JAM
44.	15	WEST COAST ALL STARS	"WE'RE ALL IN THE SAME GANG"	W B
45.	-	MONIE LOVE	"MONIE IN THE MIDDLE"	W B
46.	49	MASTER ACE	"MUSIC MAN"	COLD CHILLIN
47.	33	MC LYTE	"CAPACCINO"	FIRST PRIOR
48.	-	DJ MAJIC MIKE	"DROP THE BASS AGAIN"	CEETAH
49.	-	SHINEHEAD	"THE REAL ROCK"	ELEKTRA
50.	-	D-NICE	"CRUMBS ON MY TABLE"	JIVE

***** BREAKOUTS *****

1.	BWP	"TWO MINUTE BROTHER"	RAL
2.	REBEL MC	"REBEL MUSIC"	POLYGRAM
3.	MC TROUBLE	"GOTTA GET A GRIP"	MOTOWN
4.	SID & B-TONN	"DEATHWISH"	RAL

10218 Georgibelle #100 • Houston, Texas 77043 • (713) 465-0325 • Fax 465-2043

Rap Pool of America's Top 50 List, February 1990. *Courtesy of Steve Fournier.*

music to DJs in untapped markets across America. Starting with thirty DJs who paid a monthly fee to be included in the pool, Fournier distributed the latest hip-hop records to these DJs. The Rap Pool of America grew to over two hundred members across the world, exclusively connecting hip-hop music to hip-hop

NEW RAP RELEASES AND REENTRIES	DATE: 2-26-90	
ARTIST	RAP TITLE	LABEL
LL COOL J	"JINGLING BABY"	DEF JAM
CRAIG G	"SHOOTIN THE GIFT"	ATLANTIC
VICIOUS BEAT POSSE	"LEGALIZED DOPE-LP"	MCA
VICIOUS BEAT POSSE	"LEGALIZED DOPE--12"	"
K.M.C. KRU	"CRAZY ABOUT U"	CURB
BOBBY JIMMY & THE CRITTERS	"SOMEBODY FARTED/HAIR OR WEAVE"	PRIORITY
SHABAZZ	"GLAD YOUR IN MY LIFE"	RCA
TECHNOTRONIC	"GET UP"	S.B.K.
EGYPTIAN LOVER	"GET INTO IT"	EGYPTIAN EMP
KID SENSATION	"I S.P.I.T."	NASTYMIX
HIGH PERFORMANCE	"HERE'S A PARTY JAM"	"
KOOL ROCK J	"TOO HIGH"	JIVE
WHITE BOY MIKE & DJ THE BOY	"SOMETHING TO DANCE TO"	"
DJ JAZZY JEFF & FRESH PRINCE	"THE GROOVE"	"
J.D. RANKS-10	"GIRLS NOWA-DAYS"	VISION
BEMASTER CLAY D	"I SEEN YOUR BOYFRIEND"	BREAKAWAY
SMILEY	"FREAKOUT"	B.P.I.
MISA	"SHAKE THE HOUSE"	MOTOWN
U.T.F.O.	"MY CUTS CORRECT"	SELECT
RAW POSSE	"PUMPED UP"	"
OMEGA FORCE	"YOU CAN MAKE IT"	"
ALAMARETTA	"CONSTANTLY FLOWIN"	KNOCK'EM OUT
DIAMOND D	"DIAMOND SEZ"	CRYSTALBALL
TONY SCOTT	"GET INTO IT"	NEXT PLATEAU
TONY ROCK	"STREET RESIDENT"	EFFECT

**************************PLEASE CHECK YOUR RECORDS**************************
ANY AND ALL RECORDS,POSTERS,HYPE SHEETS,ETC... MUST BE SENT TO:
  THE RAP POOL OF AMERICA C/O STEPHEN M.J. FOURNIER 5311 KIRBY SUITE 204
  HOUSTON,TEXAS 77005 PHONE:713-522-1612
      PLEASE JUST DOUBLE CHECK FOR ME, THANKS! STEVE

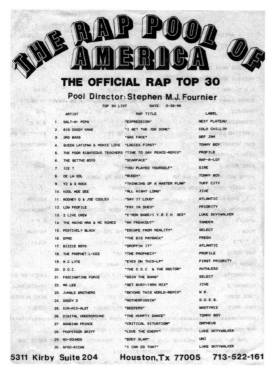

DJs and hip-hop fans.[170] The Rap Pool of America opened offices in New York and Los Angeles by 1988 and also helped Fournier become a regional representative for Def Jam Records.

With the combination of Houston's nightclubs, Kidz Jamm and greater purchasing access to hip-hop music, by 1986, Houston was a major supporter of hip-hop culture. However, Houston's hip-hoppers were still only consumers of what they received from the East Coast and other rising local sounds. Although record label executives and Nelson George had taken notice of the phenomenal consumer base of Houston, the city had yet to produce its own professional artists who could chronicle the urban realities of young people in Houston. However, within the next five years, Houston hip-hop culture would earn a spot on the hip-hop map

Top: Rap Pool of America's New Rap Releases and Reentries, February 1990. *Courtesy of Steve Fournier.*

Left: Rap Pool of America's Top 50 List, October 1990. *Courtesy of Steve Fournier.*

```
                    THE RAP POOL OF AMERICA
          POOL DIRECTOR/OWNER: STEPHEN M.J. FOURNIER
       2379 BRIARWOOD BLVD. #131   HOUSTON, TEXAS 77077
             (713) 531-7970     FAX (713) 531-8148
       OFFICE HOURS: TUES.- FRI.  9:00 AM - 5:00 PM (CENTRAL TIME)


DEAR APPLICANT:

First of all, thank you for wanting to be part of what will soon be the largest
pool in the country, and the first and only Rap Pool in the world. Plus knowing
that all of the members of The Rap Pool of America are RAP FANATICS like your-
self, should make The Rap Pool of America stronger than any other pool in
existence.

Here is some general information about the pool you shouldknow! There are only
250 slots open at this time for the entire country, so membership will be on a
first-come, first-serve basis. We carry a 25 person waiting list.... and
that's all! If you know someone who needs an application, please make a copy of
yours before you fill it out.  The Rap Pool of America will only service you
with RAP music and Hip-Hop product.

Here are just a few of the Rap labels that we have already guaranteed service of
250 copies or more.  Def Jam Records, Tommy Boy Records, Jive Records, Next
Plateau Records, Polygram Records, MCA Records, Precise Records, Sleeping Bag
Records, Select Records, First Priority Records, Sire Records, Cold Chillin'
Records, Uni, Fresh, Ruthless, Capital, Luke Records, Urban Rock Records,Rap-
A-Lot, and many more.  These are just a few of the RAP labels that have realized
the benefit of being part of The Rap Pool of America.  Knowing that 250 Rap DJs
will be waiting desperately to play their product, rather than shipping out 1000
to 2000 copies across the country, not knowing who really gets the Rap, who's
playing it, if they even like Rap. Well, this will end all of that because, as
mentioned above, all of the members of The Rap Pool of America are Rap Fanatics.

The records will come to you once every 3-4 weeks,by U.P.S., from all labels
servicing the Pool. Your first shipment should arrive about 3 to 4 weeks after
application is received.

Please fill out the application fully and send it back as soon as possible.
Remember, there are only 250 slots for the entire country!

Once again, thank you for your interest in The Rap Pool of America.  If you have
any questions, please feel free to contact me at (713) 531-7970.

Sincerely yours,



Stephen M. J. Fournier
Pool Director
```

Rap Pool of America application letter. *Courtesy of Steve Fournier.*

as artists and rap labels began to appropriate hip-hop and professionalize the local scene. But their successes would not have been possible without these significant systems of support that contributed to the aspirations for Houston to rap back.

chapter 4
IT'S TIME TO HUSTLE

HOUSTON RAPS BACK AND PROFESSIONALIZES
ITS HIP-HOP CULTURE (1986–91)

Texas is centrally located in one of the biggest hip-hop markets. There are tons of
local groups here, and I think acts like the Geto Boys, Jazzie Redd, or R.P. Cola are
competitive with New York and Philly but don't have the national exposure. Hey, New
York is where it was born, but the rest of the country has something to contribute.
—Steve Fournier, 1988[171]

In 2007, Brooklyn, New York native Talib Kweli joined forces with Port
Arthur, Texas's UGK on the rap song "Country Cousins" to juxtapose
the early development of hip-hop from two places: New York and Houston.
In a broad sense, Talib and UGK argued that hip-hop culture from all
over was connected through collective urban experiences and through the
aesthetic expression of these experiences. In a narrow sense, each artist
used the musical bars to explain how they came to participate in hip-hop
culture. Yet it was Bun B's verse that poetically summarized how artists from
Houston and surrounding areas accepted and participated in old school hip-
hop culture—by way of New York and, later, Los Angeles and Compton—
but also how they began to appropriate and contribute to the culture:

Growing up in PA, I knew nobody out there talked like us
Nothin' but that county slang, "What up dog? What up cuzz?"
Late night you see us guzzling 40s, menthols, wine, and weed
Sitting on the back porch, getting zooted, feeling fine indeed

Listening to Eric B. & Rakim or EPMD
Cool C and Steady B, plus that Public Enemy
Not to mention N.W.A., DJ Quick, and MC Eight
Down south we listen to it all, we didn't discriminate
Then along came Geto Boys, Raheem, and the Royal Flush
Rap-A-Lot Records based out in Houston represents for us
O.G. Style, The Convicts, Def IV and Too Much Trouble
Odd Squad, and Gangsta N-I-P put it down for H-Town on the double
So I said, "It's time to hustle," got down with my brother C
Put together UGK, and shit, the rest is history
We make hits by the dozen, put it down when they said we wasn't
Trust me, it's nothin—just another day in the life for country cousins.[172]

Bun B's lyrical explication is the story of many Houston hip-hoppers coming of age in the early to mid-1980s—those who became fans of hip-hop culture, participated through Houston's various systems of support and soon transitioned from dilettantes to professionals. Stories like his offer an exceptional prologue to explain how Houston's hip-hop community transitioned from supporters and participators to appropriators.

The years 1985 and 1986 were important ones for the professionalization of Houston's hip-hop culture. Most Houston hip-hoppers consider these years as the period when the first Houston rappers put their amateur skills on wax for local and regional consumption. Three singles—"MacGregor Park," "Rockin' It" and "Car Freak"—came out in that time, and these singles are regarded as Houston firsts.[173]

In the 1980s, many black families congregated on weekends at one of two local parks: Duessen Park, in northeast Houston, and MacGregor Park, in south Houston. These two parks were the host sites for picnics, barbecues, pickup basketball games, juvenile fun, quality family time and, sometimes, fights and pistol play.

Additionally, these parks were the sites of impromptu car shows and "parking-lot pimping."[174] Many young men slowly drove their upgraded old-school cars through the park lanes, showing off their pimped-out rides. These improvements were usually in the form of lowered frames (lowriders), hydraulics, high-gloss paint jobs, new rims or whitewall tires, reupholstered interiors and sound systems that made the trunk rattle because of the intense bass. If not an upgraded car, there were also guys riding through lanes showing off a new car or truck. The ride and all of its embellishments personified grandiloquence—the car was a status symbol. Moreover, men

Cover from the "MacGregor Park" single. *Courtesy of Sascha Nagie.*

used the cars to impress friends and attract women, and women viewed the man's car as a form of financial security.

This experience became the content for what is considered the first rap single from Houston, "MacGregor Park." Luscious Ice recalled, "All it talked about [was] this cat hanging out at the park, 'My car, my freak, and me.' [MacGregor Park]—that's where everybody was going on Sunday. I don't care what part of Houston you lived in. MacGregor Park was the hot park in Houston for a long time."[175] The chorus of "MacGregor Park" alone served as an ode to the good times and happenings at the park:

> *MacGregor Park*
> *Is where I got to be*
> *MacGregor Park*
> *My car, my freak, and me*

MacGregor Park
There ain't no time to waste
MacGregor Park
Because on Sundays, it's the place
Yall know

The artist of "MacGregor Park" went by the name L.A. Rapper and in his rap claimed to be a member of the Hollywood Crew. The liner notes on the album gave credit to Robert Harlan for performing and writing the song. Production credit was given to Robert Hicks and Royce Glenn Smith II. Research on the studio's address suggests that the artist, Robert Harlan, and the producer, Robert Hicks, are the same person.

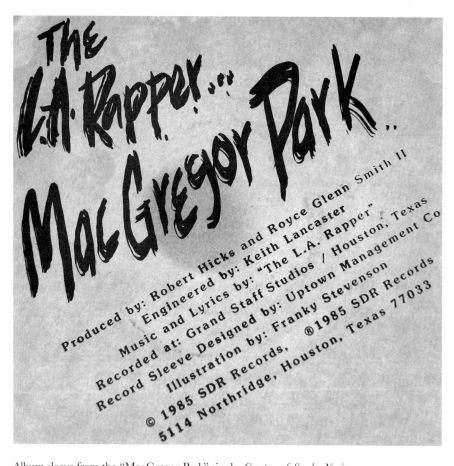

Album sleeve from the "MacGregor Park" single. *Courtesy of Sascha Nagie.*

The production of the single was reminiscent of the electro-funk (electro-hop) style popular in the early 1980s from Los Angeles artists (e.g. Egyptian Lover's "I Need a Freak" and Newcleus's "Jam On It").[176] It was fitting for the musical time, but aside from the content, it did not have a unique Houston sound.

In the four verses of the song, the L.A. Rapper explicitly represented his space and place. He highlighted Houston's car culture, chronicled the joys of hanging out at MacGregor Park, displayed the timeless mistrust that urban youth have of police officers, announced and bragged about his posse and discussed his taste for a particular type of woman. His rap placed him at the center of the world, with everything else revolving around him.[177] "MacGregor Park" told a story about a weekly hangout spot that hundreds of people were familiar with. It's a song about Houston from a Houston rapper that only Houstonians could understand. "MacGregor Park" was distributed throughout Houston and played on KTSU's Kidz Jamm, but nothing was heard of the L.A. Rapper after this 1985 single.

The next single within the triumvirate was "Rockin' It," recorded by a group of teenagers who called themselves Real Chill. Real Chill members K-Rino, Timothy Hood (G.T.) and James Conner (Preppy Jay) were South Park residents and Sterling High School students. "Rockin' It" also had an electro-hop sound, but its content was reminiscent of Run-D.M.C.'s "Sucker MCs." K-Rino, G.T. and Preppy Jay traded lyrics between bars boasting about their lyrical dexterity—their skillful ability to "rock a mic."[178] "Rockin' It" did not garner many record sales, but according to K-Rino, it was played on Kidz Jamm and allowed the group to travel around the country to perform while they were still in high school. "Rockin' It" was the first and last venture for Real Chill. Within the next two years, K-Rino continued to hone his skills through battle rapping. One such battle rap "occurred one afternoon at a neutral location known as the Battleground [a parking lot at MLK and Bellfort] against another notorious rapper from South Park, Gangsta N-I-P, [that] resulted in a draw," described Lance Scott Walker. But this same contest brought about the merger of two rap posses forming one of Houston's first rap cliques—the South Park Coalition.[179]

"Car Freaks" was the last of this group of firsts. It was a sophomoric song that rapped about women who were interested in guys only because of their cars. In it, the Ghetto Boys boasted about their ride and the beautiful dame who rode in their car—only to realize that she was in the car for superficial desires. Thus, the girl was labeled a car freak because she fulfilled her obsession for status by riding with any guy who had nice wheels.

Real Chill's "Rockin' It" vinyl single. *Courtesy of K-Rino.*

Of the first three hip-hop albums created from Houston artists, "Car Freaks" held the greatest significance—not because the song was aesthetically superior to its predecessors, but because it set the stage for Houston's version of the Sugar Hill Gang—the Geto Boys (then the Ghetto Boys)—and for the reign of Houston's Rap-A-Lot Records.

James Smith founded Rap-A-Lot in 1986 as a result of an agreement he made with two teenagers, Keith Rogers and Oscar Ceres.[180] Rogers and Ceres constantly skipped school to hone their rapping skills by visiting other schools and neighborhoods to challenge any willing contender. In a bold effort to professionalize their amateur act, they pursued Smith as a financier. Smith promised them that he would finance an album for them if they became good students. "Accepting his challenge, upon completion of their homework, the duo [met] Prince daily at the home of Prince's mother. They eventually teamed with Smith's stepbrother, Thelton Polk (K9/Sir Rap-A-Lot), to form the original Ghetto Boys. Soon afterward, Smith found himself getting 'deeper and deeper' in the music business."[181]

Much of Smith's life prior to the incorporation of Rap-A-Lot is unknown. Like Don Robey before him, Smith was raised in Houston's Fifth Ward, the eldest of five children. He came up watching his mother work hard to provide for the family, and he also witnessed much of the squalor and violence that earned the Fifth Ward the moniker the "Bloody Nickel." It was his mother's struggles and the dark realities of the Fifth Ward that inspired him to find a way to get out and make money.[182] He began working at eight years old, and after graduating from high school, he worked as a bank teller and insurance clerk. "All the while, [Smith] held a vision of something better for himself and his family. After being laid off from his insurance position, he took a job as a car dealer. He quickly noticed he had a way with people. They trusted him, opened up to him—and Smith [found success]."[183]

Since his life before Rap-A-Lot is undocumented, it is not clear how Smith financed the startup label and its production activity. However, over Smith's lifetime in the entertainment industry, numerous allegations have linked Smith to drug trafficking and other acts of criminal vice (suggesting that these activities funded Rap-A-Lot's early efforts). Despite these unsubstantiated claims, Smith is lauded by many entertainers, politicians and community leaders for his numerous acts of community service and charity in the Houston area and for his pioneering efforts to make Houston a hip-hop city.

A few other details about Smith and Rap-A-Lot remain unknown. Somewhere between the company's founding and its early 1990s success, Smith began going by the name of James Prince. It is not clear what prompted this name change, but it is known that Prince was the last name of his father, Earnest Prince III. Also, there are claims that veteran entertainment promoter Daryel Oliver co-founded Rap-A-Lot, yet no official report has ever substantiated this claim.[184] Oliver was listed as the producer on the liner notes of "Car Freaks" and was also listed on promotion material as a contact person for booking. Most records give credit to Cliff Blodgett, "a white computer software engineer from Seattle," as being a co-founder of Rap-A-Lot; however, the details of how this came about are unknown.[185] What is revealed through the research is that the efforts of Thelton Polk, Keith Rogers and Oscar Ceres played a huge role in Rap-A-Lot's founding and its initial success.

Thelton Polk, the stepbrother of James Smith, grew up in Houston's Fifth Ward and Trinity Gardens. Like other young people in the early 1980s, Polk began rapping because he was influenced by what he saw and heard coming out of New York. While a student at M.B. Smiley High School, he competed and performed in talent shows with Lester "Sir" Pace. Not long after being exposed to hip-hop and battling at his high school, Polk began to seriously pursue rap as a viable career.

In 1981, Polk performed at Houston's Kool Jazz Festival, held at Emancipation Park in the Third Ward and presented by Skipper Lee Frazier. Thelton received an award for his great performance at the festival. The next year, he and his group, the C.C. Gang, signed a one-year recording contract with the Houston Connection Recording Corporation, run by Harvey Lynch. The Houston Connection Recording Corporation was also the home of the Houston funk quartet Glass, featuring John Williams (Mikki Bleau), who were trained under Conrad Johnson at Kashmere. According to Polk, the company closed before the release of their music. Polk next relocated to the Bay Area, where he recorded and performed with Bill Summers and Band. Polk was a rapper and break-dancer with the group. He claimed that while working with the band, he learned valuable studio and recording techniques and that in 1984 he performed at the Youths Against Drug Abuse Rally at San Francisco State University. Before returning to Houston, Polk began battle rapping at Bay Area nightspots and worked with Scott Roberts of the Freaky Executives Band.[186]

Polk moved back to Houston in 1985 and began enhancing his rap skills by participating in contests at local nightspots such as the Rhinestone Wrangler, Cartoons, Gucci's, the Thunderdome, Flashes and Super Skate. Polk was one of the best battle rappers in Houston at the time. When his brother decided to enter the rap industry, he chose Polk to join the first group and chose one of Polk's aliases, Sir Rap-A-Lot, as the name of the company.

Oscar Ceres was an ambitious young rapper who often went to any lengths to show off his rhyming skills, even skipping school to battle a lyrical foe at another school. His fondness for rapping morphed into an obsession. One day, Ceres skipped school and hopped on the Houston Metro headed for Jack Yates with the intent to battle Prince Ezzy-E. While there, he caught the attention of another student and rapper by the name of Keith Rogers. Rogers befriended Ceres, and their mutual interests led them to battle others and consider rapping as a viable profession.[187]

Keith Rogers shared the ambition of his new comrade. In the early 1980s, Rogers and three other classmates—Shannon (Kid Fresh), Boyd Lee Woodberry (Rappin' Lee) and John Williams (Diamond T)—formed the group called The Awesome 3 and Jukebox. Rogers recalled that they went to great lengths to establish themselves in Houston. They caught the bus to other schools to make it in time for lunch. They were so dedicated that they created shirts that read "The Awesome 3 and Jukebox," and as Rogers boasted, "they knew what we was coming for."[188]

The Awesome 3 and Jukebox soon began to perform at college shows and other talent events. They were initially managed by the TSU chapter of Alpha Kappa Alpha sorority, which helped them get gigs and brought them along to community service events. These young ladies brokered the opportunity for The Awesome 3 and Jukebox to open up for the SOS Band at the TSU homecoming. In the audience that day was a "con artist" by the name of Brian, whose deception led Rogers and Ceres to James Smith. Rogers recalled the incident:

> *This guy Brian came to us with a briefcase and this and that. His credentials was tight, at least they looked tight to a lil' fourteen-year-old kid, and it looked like he had his act together. And my thing was RUN D.M.C.—I'm trying to get on TV…I wanna be like L.L. [Cool J]. But what he really wanted was to use us to get to the money—James Smith had the money. So he took us to meet Prince, Smith at the time, and from what I understand, Prince gave him a few thousand dollars, and we never saw him again.*[189]

This hoax did not deter Rogers. He was "so hungry that [he] never stopped going to the Fifth Ward."[190] The other members of the group began to pursue other interests, but Rogers was determined to become a rapper. He walked and caught the bus frequently to the Fifth Ward to convince James Smith to make him an album. One day, he brought his new buddy Oscar Ceres with him, and this meeting changed the trajectory of both of their lives. Ceres recalled:

> *Box called me and let me know that some individuals were interested in doing some music. So he said, "Meet me on Delia," which was in Fifth Ward, and I caught the bus out there. And when I caught the bus out there…I rapped for these individuals, and they liked how I sounded, so they introduced us to J [James Smith]. And from that point forward, the rest was history.*[191]

Rogers's recollection of the incident was similar. He claimed:

> *A few times, Prince tried to run me off, but I brought Raheem [Oscar Ceres] with me one day. I was beatboxing, and Raheem was rapping.*

[It was like on] *Krush Groove when L.L. busted through the door...well,* [we] *busted through it, and I'm beatboxin' and Raheem's rappin', and then he looked at us and said, "Yall got a deal."*[192]

Rogers continued to profess:

I am the original Ghetto Boy because I'm the one who inspired James Smith to invest his money in the music business. I believe he was going to go another direction with his money. So when I came along, he told me, "Man, if you go to school and do what you supposed to do, I'll make you a record." I went to school, and we made a record, and here we are today.[193]

In 1985, Sire Jukebox and Raheem were paired with K9/Sir Rap-A-Lot to form the group Ghetto Boys. Raheem initially proposed another group name, the Hip-Hop Vigilantes, but K9 suggested Ghetto Boys, and his stepbrother, James Smith, agreed. In 1986, the Ghetto Boys wrote and recorded "Car Freaks."

Raheem (left) and Sire Jukebox (right) at Rainbow Roller Rink. *Courtesy of Carlos Garza (DJ Styles).*

The Ghetto Boys' initial offering was played on Kidz Jamm and in local clubs, and it allowed the group to perform at local and regional concerts. But within the next three years, the group began to face challenges. Raheem decided to become a solo artist after he became disillusioned with the direction of the group. In 1987, K9/Sir Rap-A-Lot went to jail for burglary, and within a year of his release, he decided to pursue a solo career. The only remaining member was Jukebox. But that did not mean the end of the Ghetto Boys or their label home, Rap-A-Lot. For the next five years, with few exceptions, hip-hop production from Houston came exclusively out of Rap-A-Lot.

Somewhere in between the release of "Car Freaks" and the Ghetto Boys' first album, *Making Trouble*, Prince moved the company to New York. There he learned more about the industry from the likes of Lyor Cohen of Def Jam Records. Cohen "inspired him by showing off the royalty checks he'd received from L.L. Cool J and Jazzy Jeff and the Fresh Prince's works. Prince grew impatient, however, and moved the company home."[194] Prince also found it difficult to gain the respect of music executives who did not believe that anything good could come from the South. But Prince, accustomed to being underestimated and marginalized, took this as motivation and soon began to establish an independent precedent for the hip-hop industry, especially southern hip-hoppers.[195]

The two years after the company's founding was a time of experimentation and imitation. The second single was not characteristically Rap-A-Lot, as it was "un-gangsta" and lacked the ghetto stories commonly featured on future albums. Similar to "Car Freaks," this new single focused on a woman, but instead of relegating the female character to the status of a freak, this time she was the object of sexual desire. The single, entitled "Sexy Girls," was written by club promoter and emcee Captain Jack and singer/songwriter Mikki Bleau.[196] In 1984, Captain Jack released his debut album, *Jack It Up*, through Houston's Grand Records, owned by Charles Bush. Within a few months, *Jack It Up* was subsequently released by ALA Records in Los Angeles.[197] "Sexy Girls" was the last recording that Captain Jack put out. In that same year, 1987, the Ghetto Boys began to make a name for themselves by performing at shows in and out of town, continuing to battle rap around Houston and even recording a commercial for the Houston Metro. Raheem claimed that their "street cred" increased once they began working with Prince, because people on the street respected Prince.[198] They were able to perform in a concert with L.L. Cool J at Delmar Stadium, and they also performed at venues in Los Angeles.

Although the group was beginning to make waves, Raheem became disillusioned. His frustrations really began with "Car Freaks" and increased during the first year of the group.[199] By the time the group began working on their debut album, *Making Trouble*, Raheem had hesitations about moving forward with the group. He did not particularly like the practice demands or the direction that management wanted to take the group; he felt stifled. As a result, he became a solo artist.[200] In the process of these happenings, and within the first two years of the label's operation, two additional groups were signed.

Collins Leysath (DJ Ready Red), from Trenton, New Jersey, originally wanted to be a professional football player, but after visiting family in Brooklyn and going to parties in the Bronx in the late 1970s, Red fell in love with hip-hop. He began DJing in Trenton in the early 1980s, taking on the name Grand Wizard DJ Ready Red. Red had a regular gig at the Capitol Roller Rink with the Def City Crew, which also featured DJ Mixx Kidd and DJ Rock the House Shock. He soon joined forces with Prince Johnny C (Jonathan Carmichael) and Brother Radee (Eddie Moses) to form the rap group the Mighty MCs. Not only did Red DJ form the group, but he also began to experiment with production.[201]

In 1987, Red came to Houston to help his sister leave a bad relationship. Red planned to stay in Houston to get his sister away from her domestic issues before transitioning to California. During his first month in Houston (January), he began to check out the local hip-hop scene at places such as the Rhinestone Wrangler. There he hooked up with another group of out-of-town hip-hoppers who went by the name the Casanova Crew. The Casanova Crew was a collection of DJs and emcees who had each moved to Houston for college or better economic opportunities. The crew originally included members Vicious Lee (Brooklyn), EZ-Cee (Brooklyn), DJ Jon B (Brooklyn) and DJ Lonnie Mack (Chicago). Once they met Red and learned of his skills, they adopted him into the crew. In quick time, the group changed its name to Def IV and began recording a demo to pursue a record deal.[202]

One night, Red participated in a DJ contest at the Rhinestone Wrangler that attracted the attention of two Rap-A-Lot affiliates—NC Trahan and Sire Jukebox. NC Trahan introduced Red to Prince at the new Rap-A-Lot office on North Shepherd in the Heights. Prince loved the Def IV demo, but he really loved the production and instrumentation created by Red. Prince signed Def IV and brought on Red as the DJ for the Ghetto Boys.[203]

The next group signed was Royal Flush. Royal Flush was led by Ricardo Royal, a brash young man who came to Houston to escape the consequences of juvenile crimes. Royal was originally from Atlantic City, New Jersey, but in 1976, his mother decided to move the family to Los Angles to start over after a failed relationship with Royal's father. Los Angeles, particularly South Central Los Angeles, was a culture shock for Royal because of the prevalent gang culture. Along with his mother and brother, he moved into a neighborhood adjacent to the black middle-class suburb known as Baldwin Hills. This same neighborhood, nicknamed "The Jungle," was also controlled by the Bloods street gang. In South Central, Royal tried to avoid the lure of gang life by playing football and break dancing, but he was soon drawn in after the murder of one of his friends by the Crips street gang. Royal immediately joined the Bloods, seeking protection and to avenge his friend's death. As a result, he became involved in various criminal acts, including trespassing, assault and attempted murder. Royal's mother also found trouble, as she was discovered working as a vocational nurse in Los Angeles under someone else's license. Therefore, in 1981, Royal's family moved to Houston seeking to start over again.[204]

Royal arrived in Houston with hip-hop already in his veins. In Atlantic City and Los Angeles, he had been a break-dancer, and while an elementary student in Atlantic City, he had heard early hip-hop mixtapes from New York. After moving back to Atlantic City for one year, Royal settled at Aldine Senior High School on Houston's north side. Though he initially did not want to rap, he began to battle rap as a way to dominate and quiet foes. He recalled that his raps were never in the form of braggadocio like much of the rap of that time; his were more vicious and gangster, with the intent to elicit fear. He claimed that he patterned his style after Jimmy Spicer.[205]

At Aldine, Royal joined a collective of battle rappers who wanted to become professionals. The group chose the name Royal Flush, and they soon began competing in talent shows and at local nightspots such as the Rainbow Skating Rink, Flashes and the Rhinestone Wrangler. The original group included Tim Johnson (Tricky T), Donald Stewart (Cowboy), Greg Taylor (Class C), Ernest Polk (Sergio Magnifico) and Ricardo Royal (Gangsta Ric). Since they were teenagers, they had to sneak into the Rhinestone Wrangler, but once on stage, they were respected because club patrons knew them from competitions at Flashes. They became known for their ability to dominate opponents in battle-rap contests because of their skill at cap rapping. Royal noted that Class C was known as the "King of Cap Rapping." They battled Jazzie Redd, Kim Davis (Choice), the Casanova Crew, Romeo Poet and many other local rappers. Royal Flush's rising fame soon caught the attention of Prince, who convinced Royal and his group to sign with Rap-A-Lot.[206]

In February 1987, K9 went to jail for a burglary case. Now the group had only Jukebox, and by the next month, Red came on board as the official DJ. Raheem, K9 and Jukebox had already started writing lyrics for the debut album before the group changed, but now left with only one official rapper, the group needed a new member to rap the parts already written. Red recruited his MC buddy Johnny C from Trenton to fill the void left by K9. The new group, consisting of Jukebox, Red and Prince Johnny C, picked up where the original members left off in preparation for the debut album. The members camped out above the car lot while preparing the album. Johnny C, Jukebox, Prince and NC Trahan worked on lyrics, and Red "began constructing tracks with his Roland 900 drum machine and a pair of Technics 1200 turntables."[207]

While making their debut album, the group met a "dwarf named Little Billy who danced at Club Flames."[208] Little Billy (Richard Shaw) emigrated from Kingston, Jamaica, in the 1970s and settled with his family in Bushwick, New York. By the age of nine, Shaw joined the Linden Crash Crew break-dancers, with whom he found solace and excitement. "At sixteen, he was sent off to Bible school in Minnesota." He came to Houston in the mid-1980s to live with his sister and brother-in-law, a Jamaican selector (DJ). In Houston, he began hanging out at local nightspots showing off his dancing skills. Once he caught the attention of Ghetto Boys members, they thought that he would be a nice addition/gimmick to their act as a hype man and dancer.[209]

During this exciting year, Cliff Blodgett and Karl Stephenson also came into the Rap-A-Lot picture. For a time, Blodgett and Stephenson both lived in Washington, where they shared a love for music, particularly rap music. In the mid-1980s, Blodgett moved to Houston to take a job as an engineer and also to shop around the demo tape that he and Stephenson had created. In a 1998 article for the *Dallas Observer*, Stephenson recalled:

> *Cliff and I put together a studio in his attic* [in Olympia, Washington], *where we combined both of our efforts. We did a demo tape that we shopped around Houston, and a little label called Rap-A-Lot Records was really into it. Cliff had moved back to Houston to look for a job, so he gave me a call and told me they were interested in flying me down there 'cause they liked the demo. So I went and stayed on top of a used car lot with the Geto Boys for about four or five years. We stayed in this really primitive living arrangement. There was an office above the used car lot. The president of Rap-A-Lot Records, James Smith, sold used cars. So me, Jukebox, Ready Red, and Raheem stayed there, pretty much roughin' it.*[210]

By 1988, Rap-A-Lot had four albums ready for commercial distribution: the Ghetto Boys' *Making Trouble*, Royal Flush's *Uh Oh!*, Def IV's *Nice and Hard* and Raheem's *The Vigilante*.[211] Prince began shopping for a distribution deal to ensure that his label's music got to a larger audience, which would yield more money and help Houston get on the map. Prince was able to make headway with A&M Records, which at that time was known for R&B and pop music. A&M Records was initially interested in all four acts, but something went wrong during a visit to Los Angeles on which the acts were showcasing their music. There are two different stories that explain what went wrong. In one explanation, writer Jamie Lynch referred to an interview conducted by Robbie Ettelson on DJ Vicious Lee

Front cover of Raheem's "Dance Floor" single. *Houston Hip-Hop Collection, Special Collections, University of Houston Libraries.*

to claim that "17-year old Raheem got too drunk before a listening party and managed to blow the entire deal."[212] Raheem indignantly disputed this claim, arguing instead that the deal was retracted because A&M did not want to be associated with the hardcore elements of Rap-A-Lot.[213] A&M Records signed only Raheem as an artist and distributed his first album, *The Vigilante*, in 1988. Hence, Raheem would later claim on his song "5th Ward," "I'm the first muthafucka with a record out of Houston," alluding to his major label deal with A&M Records.[214]

Raheem described this album as commercial because the production team wanted a safe record that would be able to compete with the mainstream hip-hop of the time.[215] He recalled that he decided on the name *The Vigilante* because he wanted to be understood as a rogue artist that would change the direction of hip-hop. He also wanted to be seen as a rapper that would spit venom on other rappers in the industry.[216] Unlike his future works, the album was virtually free of expletives, but that did not mean that Raheem's lyrics were innocuous. Within ten songs, Raheem dissed popular rappers, including L.L. Cool J; rapped about a girl that he lost because he did not have money; petitioned for peace and the avoidance of drugs; represented his adopted neighborhood (Fifth Ward); and warned potential foes. In a *Los Angeles Times* article entitled "No Hick Jokes, Please," Dennis Hunt reported that Raheem had a "chip on his shoulder as big as Texas." He went on to suggest that East Coast and West Coast rappers did not respect "the kid from Texas."[217] Raheem did not like this. He lamented, "Rappers from New York and L.A. were saying Texas rappers ain't about nothin' and that we're stereotyped as country folk. We're not hicks. Houston rappers are tough. Houston has some great rappers."[218]

For this album, Raheem performed across the country on a promotional tour with other A&M artists, namely Shanice Wilson and Jeffery Osborne. Although his album sales are unknown, Raheem claimed that Houston showed him love because he was a local artist helping to put Houston on the map. Yet this would be his last official album for A&M Records, as the label did not know how to appropriately direct the career of a rapper. He put out his next album four years later on Rap-A-Lot. Between the time of his first album and his second release, Raheem worked on his skills as a rapper and recorded a few more singles for A&M before his contract ended.

Without a distribution deal for the other three acts, Rap-A-Lot independently distributed *Making Trouble, Uh Oh!* and *Nice and Hard*. These independent releases did not garner much commercial success. At that time, Texas did not have many distribution channels for rap music.[219] However,

Back cover of Raheem's "Dance Floor" single. *Houston Hip-Hop Collection, Special Collections, University of Houston Libraries.*

locals loved the music because the guys represented Houston. None of these releases had a uniquely Houston sound. In fact, the artists imitated the popular styles of New York rappers like Run-D.M.C. because Houston was still trying to find itself within hip-hop music.

Although it was stylistically similar to popular rap coming out of New York at the time, *Making Trouble* featured several tracks with content that displayed the group's desire to represent the place, space and lawless activities of the Fifth Ward. Jukebox claimed that the group was encouraged to be stylistically like what was popular but on occasion to write "reality" tales of life outside of the law. This made the album a special mix of braggadocio tracks and hardcore tracks. The braggadocio tracks included "I Run This," "One Time Freestyle," "Ghetto Boys Will Rock You" and "You Ain't Nothin'." On these songs, the members boasted about their lyrical prowess, bragged about the skills of their DJ and warned other rappers to stay away. The hardcore tracks include "Making Trouble," "Snitches" and "Assassins." These tracks offered vivid details of robbery, rape, carrying guns, what happens to snitches and murder. *Making Trouble* also featured two songs in response to social and political issues: "Why Do We Live This Way?" and "No Curfew." "Why Do We Live This Way?" was a solo rap that Red created before becoming a member of the group. On this song, he questions his existential realities and the social and criminal conditions of his community. "No Curfew" was partially written by K9 before his jail time. On this song, the members show their disdain for the recent curfew ordinance enacted by the City of Houston. In terms of production, Red, a connoisseur of all types of music, used many "high-profile samples that would never fly these days ('Ghetto Boys Will Rock You' used Jimi Hendrix's 'Purple Haze' guitar intro, while 'You Ain't Nothin'' lifts the guitar riff and vocal hook from Elvis' 'Hound Dog')."[220]

Though this album was stylistically imitative, the Ghetto Boys did contribute something to hip-hop culture. Red was the first person to make Tony Montana from the movie *Scarface* sing. "Four of the record's eleven tracks feature Scarface samples—sound bites of Pacino's Tony Montana saying things like, 'All I have in this world is my balls and my word' and 'Say hello to my little friend'—including the rap-less 'Balls and My Word,' which was built entirely around snippets from the film."[221] Red recalled that while working on the album, he and Little Billy were watching *Scarface* and that when they heard Pacino's famous sound bites, they both had an "aha" moment.[222] This contribution is significant to hip-hop because for a long time, Tony Montana was the model gangsta that hip-hoppers lauded, rapped about and tried to emulate. References to Tony Montana and *Scarface* were rampant in gangsta rap throughout the 1990s and the early part of the twenty-first century. Ironically, these samples appeared on Ghetto Boy songs before the rapper who would become known as Scarface joined the group.

From *Making Trouble*, the Ghetto Boys were placed on the Fat Boys' Wipe Out tour, and they toured the country performing with Public Enemy and MC Hammer.[223] Their album was also played on Kidz Jamm, and they were featured in *Right On* magazine, in which the author penned, "As the sound of rap rose up from the Bronx and spread, little did we know that hip-hop would take root in Houston. Ready or not, make room for the Ghetto Boys."[224]

Unlike the caustic battle raps that they became famous for at the Rhinestone Wrangler, Royal Flush's album *Uh Oh!* was watered down for commercial appeal. Once the group signed on to Rap-A-Lot, they thought that they would produce content focused on them shaking up the rap game and also stories of drug dealing—that is why they named the album *Uh Oh!* Royal recalled how things changed:

> [We named the album Uh Oh, thinking,] *"Y'all done fucked up— we some terrorists. We fixing to come in this rap game, and we fixing to bring what we do to records. We fixing to dis everybody, we fixing to tear niggas' asses up with our style of rap."* They wasn't having that.[225]

Their management admonished them not to curse on any of the songs, as they felt that the music would not sell because consumers were not ready for hardcore gangsta stories. They were also advised to remove all references to drug dealing out of their songs so that they would not incriminate themselves (at the time, Royal had begun selling drugs to support himself because his mother was in jail in Gatesville). As a result, Royal, who did most of the writing and production for the album, switched up the group's style and changed much of the content—taking out most of the hardcore lyrics and drug-dealing stories. From the album, Royal Flush toured with the other Rap-A-Lot acts across the Midwest and East Coast. While on the East Coast, he claimed that they performed on the show *Dance Party USA*. After returning from tour, Royal regretfully asked to be released from the Rap-A-Lot contract because he believed a rumor that Rap-A-Lot showed loyalty only to acts from the Fifth Ward. Prince allowed Royal Flush to exit their contract.[226]

In the same year that Rap-A-Lot released albums from its first four acts, a group of teenagers from Port Arthur began playing around with the idea of rapping as a profession. The group became known as the Underground Kingz but was more commonly referred to as UGK. The group went through two early transformations before becoming UGK. Mission Impossible was the name of the first group, which consisted of Chad Butler and Mitchell Queen. Chad, whose father was a trumpet player, was a band kid who played many instruments. Later, Bernard Freeman, whose childhood nickname was "Bunny," and Jalon Jackson joined the group, which led to a new name, 4 Black Menacesters. Queen and Jackson eventually quit the group to focus on their athletic pursuits. The remaining members, Chad Butler and Bernard Freeman, decided to pursue rap as full-time careers, thus forming the Underground Kingz.[227]

During this time, UGK recorded a few songs designed for a demo. The production was handled by Chad Butler (Pimp C), who also wrote lyrics,

UGK promotional picture, early 1990s. *Houston Hip-Hop Collection, Special Collections, University of Houston Libraries.*

and Bernard Freeman (Bun B) wrote lyrics. By 1991, they were spending more time in Houston attempting to professionalize their amateur act (Bun B actually moved to Houston to live with his father). One day while hanging out at Kings Flea Market in Houston's South Park, they noticed that a record shop owner had a sign posted to recruit rap acts. Russell Washington was the owner of Big Tyme Records. Pimp C and Bun B took their demo to Washington, who "fell in love with their track 'Tell Me Something Good,' a hip-hop spin on Rufus and Chaka Khan's Stevie Wonder–penned 1974 hit." Big Tyme signed the Underground Kingz, who became UGK and put together a six-track cassette called *The Southern Way*, which featured some songs that included Queen and Jackson rapping.[228] UGK would go on to be one of the most recognized and influential groups from Houston, their adopted city.

After the mediocre success of *Making Trouble*, the Ghetto Boys began working on their sophomore album. Before recording a full album, they released the single *Be Down*, which featured two new songs written primarily by Prince Johnny C and Red: "Be Down" and "My Musician."[229] These tracks introduced enhanced storytelling and enhanced production by Red. By this time, Richard Shaw transitioned from Little Billy to Bushwick Bill, yet he still was not a rapper for the group. The Ghetto Boys then began work on their seminal album, *Grip It! On That Other Level*, and in the process experienced a dramatic change that helped to solidify their identity in the world of hip-hop. Two members decided to pursue solo careers, and two new members were added to the group, giving the Ghetto Boys a more hardcore edge.

The first person to leave the group was Johnny C. Despite increased writing responsibility, Johnny C did not like the direction the group was taking through the ghostwriting of Willie D. Willie D, who had just been signed to Rap-A-Lot as a solo artist, penned two songs for the Ghetto Boys' upcoming album: "Do It Like a G.O." and "Let a Ho Be a Ho." Johnny C did not like this type of rap and decided instead to pursue a solo career and stay with Rap-A-Lot as a producer. On the first night of recording, Jukebox also decided that he did not like the new direction, so he regrettably chose to leave the group.[230] In an NPR interview, Prince commented on these departures:

> *The members were different. In the beginning stages, I let the other guys write with their own visions because I didn't have the time* [to give them input]. *I was in another business trying to make money. But eventually I*

had invested so much money into the group that I came to a stage where I said, "This is my last piece of money, and I'ma do this my way." That became a problem with the [original members] *because they felt like my lyrics, the subject matter that I wanted them to write about, was too deep. So I got rid of all of them and got people that was willing to make my lyrics that I was writing rhyme. I wasn't a rapper, so I couldn't make raps rhyme or nothing, but I had subjects and different events that I was way more familiar with than the rappers were. I think* [the move in another direction] *had a lot to do with Fifth Ward, our hood. We were only holding a mirror up to things that we had lived through in our surroundings, which are the same* [things] *that exist in ghettos around the world. So it was easy for people to embrace our subject matter.*[231]

Growing up, Willie D thought that he would either be a boxer or do something in the music industry. He began boxing as a middle school student. Willie D's uncle, Melvin Dennis, was a middleweight boxer who once fought on national TV with Wilfred Benitez. This influenced him to use boxing as a way out of the hood. But Willie D became a "stick 'em up kid" as a teenager because, as he recalled, he needed money, and boxing did not pay for food to end his stomach pains. Consequently, his offenses landed him in jail as a juvenile. After he got out of jail, he began to take rap more serious as a viable career option. Between 1985 and 1987, Willie boxed and worked for the *Houston Chronicle*, but mostly he honed his skills as a rapper. He quickly rose through the battle-rapping ranks to become known across the city as a top cap rapper.[232]

Willie and Prince shared the same barber at Harvey's Barbershop in the Fifth Ward. The barber was very impressed with Willie's rapping skills, so much that he often suggested that Willie reach out to Prince for a shot at a record deal. Willie was initially reluctant, but after constant requests from his barber, he agreed to allow his number to be passed on to Prince. Willie knew of Rap-A-Lot, but he did not think to pursue a deal with the label because he wanted to be discovered. He felt that everyone in Houston knew who he was, so if Rap-A-Lot wanted him, they would call. He also wanted to pursue a record deal with a company from New York or the West Coast. A few weeks after Prince received Willie's number, he called him in for an audition. Prince was so impressed with Willie's skills that he signed him as a solo artist. Once Prince heard what Willie wrote for his solo project, *Controversy*, Prince asked him to write some material for the Ghetto Boys' next album.[233] "Taking the group's name to heart, Willie came up with material that dealt with the lives of 'ghetto boys'—hard, grimy street tales delivered with intensity and explosive anger."[234] Roni Sarig reported:

> *As Willie began introducing new rhymes to group members Jukebox and Prince Johnny C—hardcore tracks like "Do It Like a G.O." and "Let a Ho Be a Ho"—*[Prince] *became more and more convinced that this was going to be the group's new style. Willie's creations went further in terms of depicting street realities in frank, hateful language than Johnny C wanted to go, so he quit the group. Prince took this as an opportunity to reconfigure his Ghetto Boys…and the first step was to make Willie a member of the group.*[235]

Although he did not want to become a member of a group, Willie acquiesced after Prince asked him to do it as a personal favor. Yet this was not the only change brewing.

Brad Jordan, originally from Camden, New Jersey, grew up in Houston's South Acres and South Park. He began his junior high school years attending Carter G. Woodson Middle School and later enrolled at Missouri City Middle School, where he befriended William Ross (Def Jam Blaster), Simone Cullins (Crazy C), Marcus Wiley and Chris Barriere (3-2). Blaster recalled that everyone at his middle school who participated in hip-hop in some form knew each other and that when a new person said that they could rap or beatbox, people would recommend them to the other people who participated. This is how Blaster met Jordan, who was a great beatboxer. Jordan later mentioned that he could also rap, and so they began hanging out in the garage of Marcus Wiley and making music.[236] Sometime before the age of sixteen, Jordan spent time in a mental health hospital in Houston because of his severe mental health issues and attempted suicides. After his time in the mental health facility, he went out on his own and began to take rapping more seriously. According to Blaster, they originally recorded music in 1987 under the leadership of Samuel Harris Jr., who owned HTown Records.[237] But in 1988, Jordan met a local drug dealer who had just created his own record label. This meeting changed the trajectory of Jordan's life forever.

Troy Birklett (Lil' Troy) started his record company, Short Stop Records, after he earned enough money in illegal drug dealing to support several businesses. He was always around music because his mother and father were musicians who performed in local nightclubs and recorded an album in the 1970s. Lil' Troy was also a band kid, and he remembered accompanying his parents to some of their gigs and playing his saxophone during their

RECORDS

TROY BIRKLETT
President

OFF: (713) 770-0064
P.O. Box 331005
PG: 612-1667
Houston, TX 77233
1-800-929-0585
"Ain't No Short Stopping Us"

Lil' Troy's business card for Short Stop Records. *Courtesy of Steve Fournier.*

intermission. Growing up in the Dead End—a section of Houston's South Park in which Martin Luther King Street dead ends—Lil' Troy decided to negotiate his scarcity and marginality by selling drugs. He eventually became a major force on the Houston drug scene, and in 1988, he decided to clean up his money and pursue his love for music by starting Short Stop Records. Short Stop was a name that he gained from his days as a corner drug dealer, as his workers and users knew not to short him on money.[238]

One of Troy's comrades from the streets, John Bido, knew of a young rapper and DJ by the name of DJ Akshen (Brad Jordan), who had been working on music with Bruce Rhodes (Grim Reaper). At the time, Lil' Troy did not have any artists signed to his label, so he decided to take a chance on DJ Akshen. He signed DJ Akshen and a few of his friends (Grim, 3-2, Def Jam Blaster) to two-year contracts.

DJ Akshen immediately began working on his debut album, *Scarface*.[239] Blaster, Crazy C and Grimm created the background music for his first song, "Scarface," by culling through stacks of old records. Blaster recalled that the drumbeat that he found was sampled from the song "Ashley's Roach Clip" (1974) by the Soul Searchers and that the bass line that Crazy C found came from "Gimmie What You Got" (1976) by Le Pamplemousse.[240] With the background track completed, they went into Ultimate Sounds Studio to record the album that included "Scarface" and "Another Head Put to Rest." The lead single, "Scarface," featured DJ Akshen rapping a story about a drug dealer who started off small but eventually rose in the business like Tony Montana—hence, in the rhyme, he said, "Call me Scarface."

Lil' Troy pushed the cassette throughout Houston by selling tapes out of his trunk. The song was popular on Kidz Jamm, and people throughout the city began to wonder about the identity of the kid rapping on the song. The song was such a sensation that it eventually caught the attention of Prince, who thought that DJ Akshen would be a great addition to the Ghetto Boys. Sarig noted that Prince had "been hearing a local track circulating called 'Scarface' by a south-side MC named Akshen, and he figured Akshen would be a perfect fit for the Ghetto Boys, given Red's arsenal of *Scarface* samples."[241] Prince and Lil' Troy negotiated a deal that led to Brad Jordan signing with Rap-A-Lot. In the book *Dirty South: OutKast, Lil' Wayne, Soulja Boy, and the Southern Rappers Who Reinvented Hip-Hop*, Jordan noted that he was warned to stay away from Prince, but he decided to join the Rap-A-Lot team and become a member of the Ghetto Boys.[242]

Many sources claim that DJ Akshen and K9 battled each other for a spot in the group. This claim was confusing for many years because K9 had already left the group when he went to jail. However, what was not reported was that when K9 was released, he wanted his spot back in the group. Prince had K9 and DJ Akshen battle at Red's apartment, and DJ Akshen came out as the victor.[243]

With the new lineup ready to go, Prince rounded up all of the members and headed for his home studio, located close to Prairie View, to record the Ghetto Boys sophomore album. Willie D recalled that the first time that he met DJ Akshen was when he was picked up in the van to head to the studio. This was also the first time that Jukebox found out that DJ Akshen had become a member of the Ghetto Boys. During the first night of recording, Jukebox decided that he no longer wanted to be a member of the group because he was uncomfortable with the writing style of Willie D.[244] Sarig provided two different accounts for Jukebox's departure: "Ready Red recalls that Jukebox quit the group because he didn't get along with Willie. As Willie recalls it, however, Jukebox quit after the first day of recording, when he received a letter from his girlfriend informing him that she was pregnant with twins. 'I heard she put some kind of voodoo shit on the letter,' Willie says, 'some perfume or pubic hairs or something. The man quit the group that night.'"[245]

The remaining members continued to work on the album without Jukebox. Willie D and DJ Akshen were originally the only two that were supposed to rap on the album, but Bushwick Bill soon transitioned from hype man and dancer to rapper. Willie D recalled that while they were hanging out in the studio one night, he heard Bushwick Bill rapping one of Public Enemy's songs, and Willie D then had an "aha" moment. He suggested to Prince that Bushwick Bill become a rapper for the group, but Prince was a little uneasy. Willie D then decided to write some lyrics for Bushwick Bill for him to perform for Prince. Willie D interviewed Bushwick Bill about his life as a dwarf and then penned exaggerated lyrics to fit what he thought it was like to be a dwarf. These lyrics became the song "Size Ain't Shit," and once Bushwick Bill performed the song for Prince, he became an official member.[246]

In 1989, Rap-A-Lot released three albums: (1) a single by Raheem called "Self Preservation" (2) Willie D's album *Controversy* and (3) the Ghetto Boys' *Grip It! On That Other Level*. Raheem's song was featured on the soundtrack for the movie *Lost Angels*. Willie D's *Controversy* was an expletive-filled album that addressed many controversial subjects of the time. On the album, Willie decried his angst with East Coast radio stations, called out racism and objectified women. Music reviewer Matthias Jost reasoned that on *Controversy*, Willie D "lyrically beat some sense into people who he thought weren't coming correct: discriminating radio stations, the media, the Grammys, Geffen Records, Rodney King, the KKK, the police, politicians, protesters, promoters, 'Parents Against Rap,' preachers who look out for their own benefit, and basically anyone talking loud and saying nothing."[247]

Contrary to common narratives, the Ghetto Boys' *Grip It! On That Other Level* was the album that propelled the group to stardom and helped put Houston on the map. *Grip It!* was significant not only because of its content but also because of its record number of album sales and the controversy that it caused. *Grip It!* was filled with couplet after couplet of misogyny, necrophilia, horror, pro-black political consciousness and gangster tales.[248] Its content was in stark contrast to much of the music of its time, but like NWA's 1988 release *Straight Outta Compton* and 2 Live Crew's *As Nasty As They Wanna Be*, it offered listeners a glimpse into black ghetto life that was unknown to most of the public. Instead of Carl Van Vechten gossiping about black ghetto life in Harlem, this time it was the ghetto's own products letting the world see some of the dark realities of the ghetto and some of the ways in which some chose to negotiate these realities—and they did so unapologetically. Just like Van Vechten's *Nigger Heaven* caused a stir and became a bestseller, the Ghetto Boy's *Grip It!* reportedly sold over one million copies in its first year and attracted much controversy.[249]

Within a year of *Grip It's* release (March 12, 1989), Prince was able to ink a deal with a major distributor—but not without controversy. Rick

Rubin, legendary founder of Def Jam Records, was very impressed with the Ghetto Boys music, so he signed them to a deal on his independent label, Def American, which had a distribution deal with Geffen Records.[250] Rubin came to Houston and met with the Ghetto Boys in Red's apartment to let them know that he wanted to put out their album.[251] He repackaged *Grip It!* by enhancing the production, removing two songs and adding three new songs. The most dramatic change, however, was the altering of the group's name. They went from being the Ghetto Boys to the Geto Boys, and their remastered album, *The Geto Boys*, became a self-titled national debut. Although Rubin was excited about the potential for the group, the folks at Geffen had a problem with the fringe content of the Geto Boys, so they decided not to distribute the album. Jon Pareles reported that in July 1990, "the company that had been contracted to press compact disks of *The Geto Boys*—the Digital Audio Disc Corporation in Terre Haute, IN—refused to manufacture the album after its quality-control staff listened to the album."[252] Geffen also decided to release Rick Rubin from his contract, which freed Rubin to pursue another distributor. The track that Geffen had the most problem with was "Mind of a Lunatic," which provided a detailed account of necrophilia. The Geto Boys were outraged by this decision. They felt that it was hypocritical and racist for Geffen to attempt censorship of their album when Geffen had recently released controversial content by Andrew Dice Clay, Gun N' Roses and Slayer. Nevertheless, Rubin brokered a deal with an old friend, George Drakoulias, who had just started working for Time Warner, for the distribution of *The Geto Boys*.[253] But this was not the end of the controversy.

Between 1989 and 1990, the Geto Boys toured across the country performing songs from the controversial *Grip It!* and *The Geto Boys* albums. The major leg of the tour kicked off in November 1990 when they were billed with Ice Cube and Too Short. However, because of their, lyrics some promoters cancelled some of the tour dates.[254]

Controversy also came in 1991, when a teenager in Kansas claimed that after listening to the Geto Boy's graphic single "Mind of a Lunatic" (written by Jukebox), he and his friends were influenced to act out some of the lyrics. The teenagers—Christopher Martinez and Vincent Perez—claimed that they were temporarily hypnotized by the lyrics in combination with the alcohol and drugs they had consumed.[255] One of the attorneys argued, "There is an imminent danger to young people getting a hold of this thing. It can literally mesmerize you from the repeated bass sounds that come from it. The words are horrible—it's about raping and killing.'"[256] Rap-A-Lot and the Geto Boys adamantly denied these claims and charged the defenses as racism. Yet this controversy and the actions of Geffen made the Geto Boys a national target for censorship, and they and other entertainers within pop culture were blamed for everything wrong with society at the time.[257]

The Source magazine gave *Grip It!* its highest rating, the Five Mic Award, but *The Source* also succumbed to the controversy surrounding the album. According to Dan Charnas, *The Source* "was set to run a full-page ad for the Geto Boys' album in their October 1990 issue, but their printer in Virginia balked at Rubin's chosen headline—'Play Pussy, Get Fucked'— because it was, as they put it, 'presented outside of any meaningful editorial context.'" Under pressure from the printer, *The Source* decided to drop the advertisement and opted to cover the rising tide of "gangsta rap" in their next issue. David Mills penned an article that investigated the "gangsta rap" trajectory of hip-hop culture and included a sidebar with the original advertisement and an explanation from *The Source* on why they decided not to print the advertisement.[258]

Though Rap-A-Lot attracted negative attention with the lyrics of the Geto Boys, it was still the go-to label in Houston. While the Geto Boys were on the road making a greater name for Houston, Rap-A-Lot signed on more acts, namely, Choice, The Convicts, O.G. Style and The Terrorists.

Kim Davis (Choice) was the first female act signed by Rap-A-Lot. She was considered the pioneer of hardcore/sexually explicit female rap, which was later made more popular by New York rappers Lil' Kim, Foxxy Brown, Trina and Nicki Minaj. Although her rap name appears on Willie D's song "I Need Some P----," from his *Controversy* album, Willie D claimed that this was a different person.[259] Prince approached Davis because he heard that she was a good rapper, and he pitted her against another female rapper to see which rapper he would choose. Davis came out on top and was signed as a Rap-A-Lot artist under the name Choice. Willie D penned lyrics for her debut album, *The Big Payback* (1991), which was mostly a female response to male claims of sexual prowess and objectification, offering emasculating and sexually explicit lyrics—thus a transfer of power.[260]

The Convicts was a concept group that combined Chris Barriere (3-2) and a New Orleans transplant, Michael Barnett (Big Mike). In 1991, they released a self-titled album, *Convicts*, which featured stories about revenge, selling drugs, a how-to guide for criminals and disdain for school—which the rappers claimed did not do anything to save people.[261] This was the first and last product from The Convicts, but each rapper continued to produce work for Rap-A-Lot and other Houston artists. At one point, they were pursued

O.G. Style at the Plex Studio. *Courtesy of Carlos Garza (DJ Styles).*

by Lydia Harris, wife of Michael "Harry-O" Harris, who at the time had a stake in Death Row Records. Big Mike claimed that he worked with Dr. Dre and also Snoop Doggy Dogg before being called back to Houston to fill in for Willie D, who left the Geto Boys in 1993.[262]

O.G. Style was a group composed of Eric Woods (Prince Ezzy-E or Original E) and DJ Big Boss that put out one album for Rap-A-Lot in 1991. Woods made a name for himself in the early 1980s as a battle rapper and through his tape that was played on Kidz Jamm. Their album *I Know How to Play Em'* was a regional hit due to Woods and Big Boss's history in the underground scene.[263] Local hip-hoppers fell in love with their singles "Catch Em' Slippin" and "Free World." "Catch Em' Slippin" was rumored to have been a battle rap directed toward Raheem.[264] "Free Word" was a story about how two guys broke out of jail to gain their freedom.

The Terrorists included members of the South Park Coalition clique, led by K-Rino. The group was composed of Edgar Lee (Egypt E) and Steven Baggett (Dope E), and in 1991, they released their debut album, *Terror Strikes: Always Bizness, Never Personal*, on Rap-A-Lot. Baggett was originally from Mississippi, but early in life, he and his family moved to Houston. He was trained as a musician through his summers spent at music camps in New Jersey. The Terrorists' debut album brought many of the South Park Coalition rappers national attention because they were featured on the album. Many of those featured went on to have their own success as solo rappers: Gangsta N-I-P, Point Blank and K-Rino.

During this same period, Houston native Rodney Lloyd Edmonson (Jazzie Redd) attracted national attention with his song "I Am a Dope Fiend."[265] This song was a solemn reflection about a friend's drug problem. It was fitting for the time, as America was in the midst of mass hysteria about the "War on Drugs." Jazzie Redd grew up in Houston's Second and Fourth Wards. He began DJing and rapping while a student at Jeff Davis High School. Upon graduating, he caught the attention of Wicked Cricket while rapping downtown on the Metro with K9. Cricket, an emcee and DJ, was a member of the Kidz Jamm crew and introduced Jazzie Redd to Lester "Sir" Pace. By 1985, Jazzie Redd was a regular on Kidz Jamm, and as the "master rapper," he featured a new rap every Saturday. In 1987, he and local radio personality Jerry "Smokin'" B (Jerry Ruppert), created Redd Smoke Records, which put out Jazzie Redd's first single, *Top Secret*.[266] The album contained two songs: "Top Secret" and "I Run This Town." "Top Secret," featuring Prince Ezzy-E, was Jazzie Redd's message to other rappers that his rapping skills were clandestine and that they could not be copied. "I Run This Town" was Jazzie Redd's claim to lyrical dominance in Houston. According to Jazzie Redd, "Top Secret" was the first rap record from Houston played on commercial/mainstream radio, Magic 102.1. This was probably due to the connections of Jerry "Smokin'" B.[267]

Two years later, Jazzie Redd was recruited to California by King Tee (Roger McBride, King T or Terry T) to record. King Tee was previously a member of the Kidz Jamm crew, where he went by the name Terry T. He spun records for the show and for a time lived with Lester "Sir" Pace and Jazzie Redd. Around 1984–85, King Tee left Houston for Los Angeles/ Compton to reconnect with his mother. King Tee soon began recording music with Mixmaster Spade (Frank Antonia Williams) and DJ Pooh (Mark Jordan). According to Jazzie Redd, a few of King Tee's early songs were written by him, with minor adjustments to fit King Tee's style. King Tee was eventually signed by Capitol Records, with whom he recorded his major label debut album, *Act a Fool*.[268] Once he arrived in California, Jazzie Redd did some writing with King Tee and hooked up with Toddy Tee (Todd Howard) to begin recording his next album. With Toddy Tee as the producer, Jazzie Redd released "Beach Girl," a song along the same vein as Tone Loc's "Wild Thing."[269] They were soon picked up by Pump Records, with whom they recorded a full album, *Spice of Life*, which featured the single "I am a Dope Fiend," written by Toddy Tee. According to Jazzie Redd, the song was a major success across the country, making top-one-hundred charts in 1991. It was initially played on the radio by Jammin' Jimmy Olson, who was a radio personality for Houston's newly created hip-hop radio station, 97.9 The Box.[270]

As the Geto Boys were recording their fourth studio album, two of their previous members went to jail, and one current member left the group. After K9 lost his spot to DJ Akshen, he moved back to Berkeley, California, for six months to work on music, but he was unable to catch a break. Upon his return to Houston, K9 claimed that he started a production company and created a new group called D-Force. According to K9, the group created a single titled "We Are Most Wanted" and traveled to the East Coast seeking a deal. Unable to fulfill his music dreams, he fell back into illegal activities that landed him in jail for a twenty-year sentence.[271] When Jukebox left the Geto Boys in 1989, he began to imitate the gangsta stories that his group had become famous for. Jukebox got involved with a neighborhood gang and in 1990 was involved in an altercation that led to the murder of a rival gang member. As a result, he was charged with murder and in 1990 began a twelve-year prison sentence.[272]

While the Geto Boys were on the road touring and making preparations for their follow-up to *Grip It!/The Geto Boys*, Red became suspicious of the accounting practices of the label. According to Red, they were performing all over but not being paid what he thought they should. After he contracted the services of an accountant and lawyer, he was viewed as a dissenter. Red tried to get the group together to present a united front against the label, but when confronted by the label, he stood alone with his complaints. Red claimed that after that confrontation, he decided to quit the group, leaving behind production work on the group's forthcoming album, as well as DJ Akshen's debut as Scarface.[273]

On the night that Red left the group, Bushwick Bill was shot in the eye in a failed suicide attempt. On May 9, 1991, Bill spent the day partying, drinking assorted alcohols and smoking marijuana. The combination of this activity and his emotional state led him to "fatal thoughts of suicide." According to Bill, he was depressed because he did not have all the things that he thought that he should have.[274] Early in the morning on May 10, he returned home to his seventeen-year-old girlfriend and her child. He begged his girlfriend to party with him, and when she refused, he asked her to shoot him. His girlfriend refused, and then Bill began to threaten to throw the infant child out the window if she did not shoot him. After that did not work, he handed his girlfriend his gun—with his hand cocked on the trigger.

A struggle ensued, and as the girlfriend tried to uncock the weapon, a shot went off, and the bullet went into one of Bill's eyes.[275] This scene was later depicted in Bushwick Bill's video for the song "Ever So Clear," which was a single from his solo album *Little Big Man*. A few days later, Bill's incident became a commercial opportunity. Sarig noted:

> *After Bill's condition stabilized, Scarface and Willie D joined him at the hospital to lend support. Some enterprising individual affiliated with Rap-A-Lot got the idea to shoot a photo of the Geto Boys in their self-inflicted glory, and so it was immortalized: Bushwick Bill, in his hospital gown and "5th Ward Posse" hat, first-generation cell phone in hand, being wheeled down the hospital hallway by a pimped-out Willie D, in a purple denim outfit, and gangsta-clad Scarface, in black leather pants and porkpie hat. The shot became the cover image for We Can't Be Stopped.[276]*

Years later, Bushwick Bill lamented the decision to commodify his incident in Brian Coleman's book *Check the Technique: Liner Notes for Hip-Hop Junkies* (2007). Bushwick noted:

> *It still hurts me to look at that cover because that was a personal thing I went through. I still feel the pain from the fact that I've got a bullet in my brain. To see that picture only brings it back more so. I think it was pretty wrong of them to do it, even though I went along with the program at first. I really didn't understand why that picture was so important for them—important enough to take the IV out of my arm and endanger my life by taking the patch off my eye. I could have been blinded for life. And Face was against it the whole time. That's why he has that look in his eye in those pictures.[277]*

A few weeks after the incident, the Geto Boys' fourth album, *We Can't Be Stopped*, was released.[278] It featured Willie D, Scarface and Bushwick Bill as the group members, and due to the album's success, this rendition of the group became the most famous. Although the album maintained some of the misogynistic, juvenile, horrifying and in-your-face lyrics that the group had become known for, it also contained moments of social commentary that showed that the Geto Boys were maturing men. The most evident example of this was the song "Fuck a War," which provided a counter narrative to the notions of American nationalism and solidarity during the Gulf War.

Within a year of its release, the album had reached over 1 million sales and had charted on both rap and non-rap music charts.[279] According to

Brian Coleman, "The group also toured more than ever before in 1991 and 1992, with hip-hop marquee acts of the day like Public Enemy, Naughty by Nature, Too $hort, Ice Cube, and Queen Latifah."[280]

For *We Can't Be Stopped*, Rap-A-Lot ended its relationship with Rubin/Def American and secured a distribution deal with Priority Records. According to Prince, Priority had the right things in place to help Rap-A-Lot be successful. Prince recalled:

> *Once I had established that I could sell records, all of the record labels that had turned me down prior was tryin' to get at me. But what was attractive about Priority was that they were an established independent with a major distribution deal but actually had people in there that knew how to work the records properly at retail. They had an edge on a lot of the record labels. So I hurried up and embraced that deal and sold a bunch of records.*[281]

Though Red was no longer in the group, he did contribute to *We Can't Be Stopped*. He was featured on the opening track of the album, "Rebel Rap Family." He also loaned the records to Scarface that were used as samples for the most popular song on the album, "Mind Playing Tricks on Me."[282] "Mind Playing Tricks on Me" was originally intended for Scarface's solo project, *Mr. Scarface Is Back*.[283] Red recalled that Scarface had started dabbling with production, so he asked Red to borrow a few albums. The two singles that he picked out of Red's crates were "Hung Up on My Baby," from the *Tough Guys* soundtrack, and "Pickin' Boogers," from Biz Markie's album *Goin' Off*.[284] "Hung Up on My Baby" was sampled for the bass line, and "Pickin' Boogers" was sampled for the drum line. "Mind Playing Tricks on Me" garnered the group its most success and became its most recognizable song. On the four verses, each Geto Boy told stories juxtaposing reality with their crazy thoughts of "paranoia and schizophrenia to loneliness, regret and depression, and finally—in Bill's Halloween ghost tale—delusion."[285] The song hit the airwaves across the nation and soon became a number-one hit, attracting more fans and more sales.

Due to the success of DJ Akshen's song "Scarface" on his Short Stop Records debut and the subsequent remake on *Grip It!*, he became synonymous with the character and thus took on the name as his rap persona. By the end of 1991, his debut album, *Mr. Scarface Is Back*, was released with great fanfare.[286] *The Source* gave the album a four-mic rating and maintained, "Geto Boys fans will flip over Scarface's effort. Simply stated, *Mr. Scarface Is Back* personifies 'hardcore gangsta shit' and hits harder than an aluminum bat. Scarface, like his Houston cohorts, has come off, making an album that takes it to yet another level."[287]

By 1991, Houston had established itself as a hip-hop city. It did so by establishing solid systems of support: (1) large nightclubs that helped thousands of people become exposed to hip-hop culture on a weekly basis and also served as the training ground for future rappers, (2) a local college radio station (that stood alone for years) responsible for breaking new music and engaging people in hip-hop culture and (3) a large consumer market that allowed Houstonians to own artifacts of the culture. With a firm base established, Houston began to professionalize its culture by rapping back.

Although there were many rappers and groups that began to record hip-hop music around 1985–86, Rap-A-Lot and its most prominent group, the Geto Boys, kicked down doors so that outsiders could see what Houston had to offer. They did so unapologetically—by telling stories unique to their space and place—and they did so independent of major label support and in the face of major opposition to their message and geography.

We Can't Be Stopped was the appropriate title for the Geto Boys' 1991 album—not only for them but also for Houston. On three of the tracks—the intro ("Rebel Rap Family"), the title track ("We Can't Be Stopped") and "Trophy"—they made a bold proclamation to their haters and detractors (e.g. other rappers, radio stations, the rap industry, Geffen, promoters, censors and politicians) that "no weapon formed against them would prosper." Yet their proclamation transcended the album and their troubles—it was also a decree to the world that something good could come from Houston, that Houston was a hip-hop city to be reckoned with and that hip-hop from Houston would continue.

AFTERWORD

Houston hip-hop continued to develop after 1991 and remains a vibrant part of the city's life today. In the early 1990s, a new sound began bubbling up in Houston's south-side neighborhoods such as Hiram Clarke, South Park, Sunnyside and the Third Ward. A young DJ named Robert Earl Davis Jr. (DJ Screw) began recording and selling distinctive mixtapes that found success as an underground craze and ultimately forged a new identity for Houston hip-hop. DJ Screw originated a production technique that used the technology of the time—vinyl records, turntables, a mixer and multiple cassette decks—to create cassette mixes of strangely slow, murky versions of existing songs punctuated with repeated words and phrases. He drew his source material from a growing record collection of primarily Houston and West Coast rap, some R&B, a sprinkling of southern and East Coast hip-hop and even funk and reggae. The style that he debuted on these tapes would become known around the world as "chopped and screwed."

To create the sound, Screw used the pitch controls on his turntables to slow down the records, or "screw" them. He also played two copies of the same record, one a beat behind the other, and used his mixer to switch back and forth in order to repeat certain sounds, or "chop." After he recorded a set, he dubbed copies from his master tape, adjusting the pitch control of a four-track cassette deck to slow the music even further. On the resulting tapes, mid-tempo beats sounded like dirges, horns sounded like the cries of elephants and rappers' voices were deep and murky. Listeners found it to be the perfect chill-out music for cruising, particularly when high.

Screw initially made these tapes as "personals" for individuals in his circle, recording requested songs and giving "shoutouts" to friends and hoods for ten dollars. Soon he was selling dubs of the tapes to a larger audience. Around 1992, emerging south-side rappers such as Courtney Smith (C-Note), Patrick Hawkins (Fat Pat), his brother John Hawkins (HAWK) and Marcus Edwards (Lil' Keke) began freestyling (improvising) over tracks, dubbing themselves—and dozens of others who appeared on the tapes—the Screwed Up Click (SUC). Now that the tapes included hot freestyles, demand increased. For a period of five or six years, DJ Screw's homemade "screw tapes" or "gray tapes" (named for the color of the Maxell cassettes he used) all but replaced radio on the south side as the source for hearing new music. The trends that the SUC freestyled about—wearing diamonds on their teeth, driving colorful custom cars called "slabs" and drinking the codeine promethazine and soft drink mixture known as "syrup"—became permanently associated with DJ Screw and the SUC.[288]

Many years later, Lil' Keke would describe how the lyrics of the freestyles reflected the concerns of a tightknit community of people, primarily d-boys (drug dealers), rappers and other friends:

> *It was really about these six or seven neighborhoods, what we were doing in these six or seven neighborhoods and the people that was havin' cars and havin' money. Everything that was happening in this circle...that's all we cared about. Everything about the beach, everything about every club, everything about everywhere we went was about these five high schools.*[289]

As Faniel has discussed, hip-hop is often intensely regional or local. This was hip-hop localism at its most extreme.

As the popularity of DJ Screw and the SUC grew, their story included both triumphs and tragedies. Many SUC members became local stars and released independent albums that sold well and often charted nationally among Billboard's top R&B/hip-hop albums.[290] They began to tour. Strong sales led to the repackaging and national distribution of albums by Lil' Keke, E.S.G. and Yungstar. A later member of the SUC, Lil' Flip, would have the greatest success of all with his albums *Undaground Legend* (Suckafree/Columbia, 2002) and *U Gotta Feel Me* (Columbia, 2004), both of which went platinum. DJ Screw released four albums of his own, including the popular *3 'N the Mornin' (Part Two)* (Big Tyme Records, 1995), and in 1998 opened a music store called Screwed Up Records and Tapes, which became a local hip-hop landmark.

But 1998 also saw the murder of SUC member Fat Pat shortly before the release of his first album, cutting off a promising career.[291] On November 16, 2000, DJ Screw himself was found dead in his recording studio from an overdose of codeine and other drugs, leaving family, friends and fans in shock.[292] Death continued to shadow the SUC: Fat Pat's brother HAWK was murdered in 2006, Big Moe died in 2007 of a heart attack and SUC affiliate Pimp C died in 2007 from sleep apnea exacerbated by syrup use.[293]

In the late '90s, fans on the north side of town—which includes the neighborhoods Acres Homes, Greenspoint, Homestead and Studewood—began demanding "chopped and screwed" style sounds from their own DJs. As one-time Swishahouse rapper Slim Thug recalled, "The north side didn't have no rap scene when Screw and them was holdin' it down. Wasn't nobody from the north rappin'."[294] Established mixtape and radio DJ Michael "5000" Watts filled the void. He and fellow DJ Ronald Coleman (OG Ron C) released slowed-down mixtapes featuring young unknown rappers from the north side and founded the Swishahouse label. In 1999, Watts and Ron C released their first aboveground album, *The Day Hell Broke Loose*, which featured early Swishahouse artists such as Archie Lee, Big Pic, Big Tiger, Larry Jones (J-Dawg), Lil' Mario and Lester Roy plus three young newcomers—Stayve Thomas (Slim Thug), Hakeem Seriki (Chamillionaire, then going by Camilean) and Paul Slayton (Paul Wall).

In 2005, a crop of artists who were either on the Swishahouse label or got their start there began to break big nationally. "Still Tippin'" by Mike Jones put Houston on the map in a way not seen since the Geto Boys' 1991 "Mind Playing Tricks on Me." "Still Tippin'" was built around a slang-filled hook that mystified the rest of the country: "Still tippin' on four fours, wrapped in four vogues...."[295] The stretched ascending notes of producer Salih Williams's "William Tell Overture" sample provided an edgy counterpoint to the drawled braggadocio of rappers Slim Thug, Mike Jones and Paul Wall. The accompanying video, played regularly on MTV and BET, introduced the country to the unique musical subculture of Houston. Rappers drawled about "84s" and "syrup sipping" as they flashed diamond "grills" (teeth jewelry) from behind the wheels of jewel-toned slabs.

Slim Thug, a six-foot-six rapper known for wearing the braids characteristic of the north side and driving a slab with longhorns on the hood, made his major label debut with *Already Platinum* (Star Trak/Geffen, 2005). It peaked at number two on the Billboard charts. Mike Jones's *Who Is Mike Jones?* (Swishahouse/Asylum/Warner, 2005) went platinum. Paul Wall, a white rapper who had a lucrative business making custom grills, earned the number-one R&B/hip-hop album of the year spot with *The People's Champ*, which featured a song that was built around a Big Pokey line from a Screw tape.[296] *MTV News* did a major feature on "chopped and screwed" and syrup.[297] While the rest of the country wasn't looking, Houston had developed its own sound, slang, fashion and even drug culture.

This culture was incubated in an organic and inward-looking way, as Houstonians were left to do their own thing while mainstream hip-hop paid little attention to them (save for the Geto Boys, whose *We Can't Be Stopped* had gone platinum in 1992). In Houston, artists tended to look to each other for musical inspiration, they were able to make a living from local and regional sales and they found homes on mushrooming independent labels, many seeded by drug money from the intractable crack trade. But they owed much to the pioneers of 1979–91—people like Steve Fournier and Wicked Cricket, who fought to play rap in Houston clubs; the maverick K-Rino, who refused to sign to a major label and chose to support fellow artists instead; and J. Prince, who combined his fierce determination and business savvy to create a blueprint for independent hip-hop labels. In a video for the song "I Ain't Heard of That," from his 2005 major label debut, young star Slim Thug nods to this lineage by wearing a T-shirt featuring the famous album cover of the Geto Boys' *We Can't Be Stopped*.

In 2007, the Grammy for Best Rap Performance by a Duo or Group went to Chamillionaire with Krazie Bone for the song "Ridin'," with its defiant hook "tryin' to catch me ridin' dirty." The song was the second single from his album *The Sound of Revenge* (Chamillitary/Universal, 2005). In an interview following the awards show, Chamillionaire conveyed the speed and intensity of his breakthrough:

> *Earlier this year, it kept on getting better and better. After I went platinum… that was real good to see a plaque finally. And then to sell 4 million ringtones—I broke some kinda record. And then I was like, "It don't get no better than this." And then Weird Al did a parody of "Ridin'," and then it was like it can't get no better than that. And then after that, I win a Grammy, so now I know it can't get any better.*[298]

During the heady heyday of the mid-2000s, mainstream hip-hop was no longer questioning the relevance of Houston.

Although this essay focuses primarily on the peculiarly local genre of "chopped and screwed," there were other important developments in Houston hip-hop from 1992 forward that led to respect and recognition for southern artists. Some of these stories overlapped with the development of screw culture, and some were distinct.

The Geto Boys continued to blaze their own trail, both collectively and in solo efforts. With the departure of Willie D from the group, their follow-up to *We Can't Be Stopped* was recorded with Big Mike of the Convicts in his place. *Till Death Do Us Part* (Rap-A-Lot/Priority, 1993) contained the single "Crooked Officer," an anti–police brutality song recorded a year after the Los Angeles riots over the acquittal of the officers who beat Rodney King. Although the Geto Boys were fierce defenders of Houston and loyal to where they came from, their lyrical attacks usually spoke to national issues: the fight over the legitimacy of rap music, the ongoing battles of African Americans against racism, provocative debates over boundaries of taste and the interior struggles of the mind.

By the mid-90s, Scarface was considered "the South's most admired rapper."[299] His 1995 solo album *The Diary* (Rap-A-Lot/Virgin) delivered a depth not often found in gangsta rap. It is highlighted by "I Seen a Man Die," with its spellbinding lyrics about the final moments of death:

> *I hear you breathin', but your heart no longer sounds strong*
> *But you kinda scared of dying, so you hold on*
> *And you keep on blacking out 'cause the post is near*
> *Stop trying to fight the reaper, just relax and let it go*
> *Because there's no way you can fight it, though you'll still try*
> *And you can try it til you fight it, but you'll still die.*[300]

In 1996, Willie D returned to the Geto Boys, and the group released one of their most well-received albums in the funky and socially conscious *Resurrection* (Rap-A-Lot/Virgin). With their loyalty to Rap-A-Lot producers such as Mike Dean and N.O. Joe, the Geto Boys were not influenced by screw music. Their last studio album was released in 2006, but they continue to tour in 2013.

Falling somewhere in between the hand-to-hand distribution of the screw tapes and the well-oiled machine that was Rap-A-Lot were numerous Houston labels that operated independently. The existence of sub-distributor Southwest Wholesale in Houston was another factor that allowed Houston artists to thrive. Southwest Wholesale sent the product of local rap labels to stores throughout the Southwest, allowing them to bypass major labels but still make money. In 2003, the company closed its doors.[301]

The South Park Coalition offered a support network for numerous independent rappers. As founder K-Rino recalls, "We started in 1987 as an organization of MCs from the South Park neighborhood."[302] Early SPC members included Gangsta N-I-P, who introduced the world to his creepy "horrorcore"; Dope E and Egypt E of the Terrorists, Point Blank; and Klondike Kat. Other rappers to join the SPC included members of the legendary early-90s group Street Military and female artist Cl'Che'.

Stories from the Black Book (Electric City Records, 1993) was K-Rino's first solo album, its title a reference to the black notebooks in which he wrote his lyrics. A conscious rapper in a gangsta city, he stands out for his lyrical style, philosophical subject matter and wicked punch lines. In 2007's "Raised in the Dead End," K-Rino put his keen eye to describing the bleak Dead End neighborhood:

> *Used to skip school to pick up street knowledge from Gs*
> *Makin' millions without diplomas or college degrees*
> *Everyday some gunfire penetrated the air*
> *You might get set up by the same chick that braided your hair*
> *If you know about some dirt, then you better not tell it*
> *The whole hood is like a flea market: you need it, we sell it.*[303]

But in songs like 2008's "Holla at Me" and 2011's "Perfect World," he offered fans something different: hope. Despite not receiving commercial radio play, K-Rino continues to build a cult international fan base via the Internet.

Carlos Coy (South Park Mexican) founded the label Dope House in 1995 with his brother Arthur Coy. Known to fans as SPM, he wove relatable stories of life in the barrio such as "Hillwood," as well as light-hearted hits such as "High So High." According to *The Atlantic*, "His first handful of albums sold more than 1.5 million units, a tremendous number for an independent artist. In 2000, he signed a deal with Universal."[304] That success inspired numerous other Hispanic musicians. In 2002, SPM was sentenced to forty-five years in prison for sexual assault on a child.[305]

Other Hispanic rappers thrived in a city where African American and Hispanic fans came together comfortably to support their favorite artists. The mid-90s saw the formation of the independent rap group Aggravated and the signing of transplanted Californian Ronnie Bryant (Baby Beesh/ Baby Bash) to Dope House.[306] Christian Garcia (Lucky Luciano) signed to Dope House in 2002 before starting his own Steak N Shrimp Records.[307] Pedro Herrera III (Chingo Bling) skewered elements of Hispanic and hip-hop culture equally in his comic raps, leading to a distribution deal with Asylum Records in 2006.[308]

In 1992, New York City–based Jive Records picked up the contract for Port Arthur's UGK and released *Too Hard to Swallow*, which included six songs from the duo's cassette-only debut.[309] UGK's appeal came from the interplay between the drawl of Pimp C and the smooth cadence of Bun B, smart lyrics that mixed Port Arthur shout-outs with grimy street stories and a dose of humor and a melodic production style developed by Pimp C that incorporated samples from '70s soul artists the Isley Brothers, Rufus and Chaka Khan and Bill Withers. With UGK, southernness was an integral part of the package.

In describing their second album, Bun B explains its relationship to screw culture:

> *Ridin' Dirty was originally created to be a studio album that felt like a screw tape. If you listen to Ridin' Dirty, a lot of the songs and tempos are slower. If you look at the artwork for Ridin' Dirty, we are literally in front of DJ Screw's house.*[310]

UGK even recorded a screw tape with DJ Screw using the beats from the album, but they were unable to convince Jive that a separate chopped and screwed commercial release would sell.[311]

UGK grew their fan base slowly and surely, with a little help from their appearance on Jay-Z's 1999 hit "Big Pimpin'." Their ascent was halted when Pimp C was sent to prison in 2002 after violating parole following an aggravated assault charge.[312] Upon his release, UGK's polished comeback album *Underground Kingz* (Jive, 2007) went to number one on the Billboard charts. In the midst of this unparalleled success, Pimp C died, leaving Bun B with the task of preserving his friend's legacy while carrying on as a solo artist.

By the mid-2000s, Rap-A-Lot found itself home to a number of successful solo acts. Both Pimp C and Bun B released solo projects on Rap-A-Lot. Funky stoner rapper Devin Copeland (Devin the Dude) put out albums every few years for a rabid audience. And two of the youngest members of the Screwed Up Click, Joseph McVey (Z-Ro) and Frazier Thompson III (Trae), achieved new levels of popularity with well-received projects like Z-Ro's bluesy *The Life of Joseph McVey* (Rap-A-Lot/WEA, 2004) and Trae's *Restless* (Rap-A-Lot/WEA, 2006). In the intervening years, Devin, Z-Ro and Trae have ended their contracts with Rap-A-Lot, and Trae has signed to Atlanta rapper T.I.'s Grand Hustle label.[313]

As a librarian in Special Collections of the University of Houston (UH) Libraries, in recent years I became interested in documenting Houston hip-hop, particularly the life and career of DJ Screw. In our repository, we hold papers of many prominent Houstonians and the records of local arts organizations, and I felt that the papers of this influential DJ who created a new genre of hip-hop belonged alongside them. By collecting hip-hop material, we could preserve an ephemeral slice of music history, provide rich sources for future scholars and bring stories of African American men into the archives. With the support of my department head and library administration, in 2010, I began actively seeking materials related to Houston hip-hop.

At this time, there was a growing interest in hip-hop studies in academia but few archival collections dedicated to hip-hop. Cornell University in Ithaca, New York, established the groundbreaking Cornell Hip-Hop Collection in 2007 to chronicle the pioneers of the Bronx. But the Houston Hip Hop Collection at UH would be the first to document local hip-hop music and culture in the community in which it was created. As the second most ethnically diverse major research university in the United States, with our main campus located near the historically African American neighborhoods of Third Ward, Fifth Ward and South Park, we were well situated to collect, preserve and make available this material.[314] Paul Wall and Chamillionaire both attended UH, and many of our students are hip-hop fans who come from the same neighborhoods as famed Houston rappers.

I knew that in order to succeed, I would need to make this effort as collaborative as possible and reach out to rappers, DJs and family members of deceased artists who could share their expertise. It was important to me to represent the music scene accurately and to get input from the community, especially its African American members. As a white librarian with little knowledge of hip-hop or its surrounding culture, I had a few reservations. How would I be perceived by potential donors? Would the rappers be as intimidating as they appeared in their videos? Could I convince people of the worth of the project? I decided to simply be myself and present myself as a student ready to learn.

Happily, the rappers, DJs and family members all responded positively to the idea of the collection. The goodwill people felt toward the late DJ Screw encouraged buy-in toward the project. Friends and family members of those artists who had died young were very helpful, welcoming the university's recognition of their loved ones. I found all of the rappers and DJs to be personable and interesting—after all, they are entertainers! Many of them grew up under difficult circumstances in rough neighborhoods, and I gained respect for the way they responded to those challenges with creativity and innovation.

In 2010, the UH Libraries acquired DJ Screw's vinyl collection from his father, Robert Davis Sr. The DJ Screw Sound Recordings include approximately 1,500 of the 5000 vinyl records owned by the DJ, most notably those used to make his mixtapes. A small set of personal memorabilia accompanied the vinyl.[315] Other donated collections include material related to the rapper HAWK, Pen & Pixel Graphics and Samplified Digital Recording Studios.[316] The UH Libraries launched the Houston Hip-Hop Collections through an exhibition and conference. "DJ Screw and the Rise of Houston Hip-Hop" (March–September 2012) told the story of the DJ through artifacts such as childhood photos and a birthday card to his longtime girlfriend, as well as musical equipment and vinyl records. The two-day event Awready!: The Houston Hip-Hop Conference (March 27–28, 2012), which we co-presented with the H.E.R.E. Project at Rice University, UH's African American Studies program and UH's Cynthia Mitchell Woods Center for the Arts, included a day of short presentations and panel discussions that brought rappers, scholars and the general public together. In order to consolidate our efforts, UH Libraries joined together with the like-minded H.E.R.E. Project to form the Houston Hip-Hop Archives Network.[317]

The vinyl records in DJ Screw's collection now sit in acid-free boxes in the climate-controlled stacks of Special Collections, each nestled in a protective sleeve. Among them are many releases by Houston artists. Rap-A-Lot is well represented with records by the 5th Ward Boyz, Big Mello, Convicts, both Ghetto Boys and Geto Boys, Raheem, Royal Flush and more. Rare test-pressings by SUC members Lil' Keke and E.S.G. are also preserved. Singles by chart toppers Lil' Flip, Lil' Troy and UGK are housed next to those by underground legends K-Rino and Street Military. The records themselves suggest the interwoven nature of Houston hip-hop—because Houston artists were largely ignored by mainstream hip-hop, they learned to look to themselves, to each other and to those who came before to create an independent and distinctive music culture that flourishes to this day.[318]

JULIE GROB
Coordinator of Digital Projects and Instruction
Special Collections, University of Houston Libraries

NOTES

INTRODUCTION

1. John Hope Franklin, "On the Evolution of Scholarship on Afro-American History," in *The State of Afro-American History*, 13.
2. Jay-Z, "Decoded: Jay-Z in Conversation with Cornel West."
3. These eras include the Old School, the Golden Age, the Modern Era, the Industrial Era and the one in which we are living now. William Jelani Cobb defined the first four eras, noting, "Art respects no borders and time frames, but for our own concerns, hip-hop can be divided into four overlapping eras: the Old School, 1974–1983; the Golden Age, 1984–1992; the Modern Era, 1992–1997; and the Industrial Era, 1998–2005." Cobb, *To the Break of Dawn*, 41.
4. Kelley and Lewis, eds., *To Make Our World Anew*, 613; Mark Anthony Neal called this generation "soul babies" in Neal, *Soul Babies*; Kelley also defined this time period as "post-segregation" in Kelley, *Into the Fire*, 7.
5. Kitwana noted, "The term 'hip-hop generation' is used interchangeably with black youth culture. No other term [in his opinion] better defines this generation of black youth, as the entire spectrum of black youth (including college students and young professionals, as well as the urban masses) has come to identify with hip-hop's cadence." Kitwana, *The Hip-Hop Generation*, xiii.
6. Dagbovie noted that Kitwana "designates the hip-hop generation as including those African Americans born between roughly 1965 and 1984 who share a common worldview concerning 'family, relationships, child rearing, career, racial identity, race relations, and politics.'" Kitwana as quoted in Dagbovie, "Black History's Relevance to the Hip-Hop Generation," 302.
7. Jay-Z, *Decoded*, 255.
8. Dagbovie, "Black History's Relevance to the Hip-Hop Generation," 301.
9. Cobb corroborated this claim in noting, "The constant blues references to crossroads, trains, and railroad tracks rise from itinerant life at the turn of the

century. Between 1920 and 1942, at least 293 blues songs about trains or railroads were recorded. This is the music of black wanderers exercising the newly granted right of mobility. And thus we encounter titles like 'Goin' Away Blues,' 'So Many Roads, So Many Trains,' 'Crossroads Blues,' and 'Further Up the Road.'" Cobb, *To the Break of Dawn*, 25.

10. Ibid.
11. Mickey Hess's claims were made in the introduction of his regional hip-hop guide, *Hip-Hop in America: A Regional Guide*. Murray Forman's claims were initially promoted in the *Popular Music* journal article in 2000 and later in his text *The Hood Comes First: Race, Space, and Place in Rap and Hip-Hop*. Arguments used in this text can be found in Forman, "'Represent'," 65.
12. Forman, "'Represent'," 73.
13. Ibid.
14. Lynch, *Hip-Hop in America*, 429.
15. Steve Fournier, interview.
16. John 1:46 (New International Version, 2011).
17. Ibid.

CHAPTER 1

18. George, *Hip-Hop America*, 2.
19. "M.K. Asante Jr. reinforced the notion that hip-hop emerges from a state of cultural convergence. As he asserts, hip-hop is forged within particular circumstances encompassing contradictory and contestational interest as well as circulating across varied media platforms, yet it is oriented toward a decidedly alternative set of values that are frequently at odds with the cultural mainstream." Neal, *That's the Joint!*, 2.
20. George, *Hip-Hop America*, 14.
21. Rose, *Black Noise*, 21.
22. See Daniel Bell's book *The Coming of Post-Industrial Society* (1973) for his definitions of a post-industrial society; Richard Scase summarized Bell's description of a post-industrial society in "Review of the Coming of Post-Industrial Society," 508–09; See Rose's characterizations and effects of deindustrialization on cities like New York, Philadelphia and Compton in Rose, *Black Noise*, 27–33; Neal, *That's the Joint!*, 478–84. See Neal's arguments for how post-industrialization and urban renewal negatively altered the communal sensibilities of black communities, and how unemployment as a result of the loss of an economic base hindered the efforts to create sustainable black communities. Neal also argued that as a result of benign neglect and fractured communities, the urban poor came to be viewed through the eyes of the commercial media as dysfunctional.
23. George claimed, "America's dark side is comprised of those who don't fit neatly into the official history—unneeded workers and uneducated youth whose contact with American government is usually limited to mean-spirited policing, their filthy abandoned neighborhoods covered up by graffiti. The suburban revolution, the one supported and celebrated by major industry (auto, oil, rubber, real estate),

along with prejudice against blacks and Hispanics, had left large chunks of our big cities economic dead zones that mocked the bicentennial's celebration of America as the promised land." George, *Hip-Hop America*, 14.

24. Grandmaster Flash and the Furious Five, *The Message*.

25. Melle Mel's lyrical diagnosis of the post-industrial Bronx can be better understood by highlighting the statistics of the southern end of the Bronx provided by Nelson George in *Yes Yes Y'all*, 3.

26. George, *Hip-Hop America*, 10.

27. Neal, *That's the Joint!*, 483.

28. John F. Szwed, "The Real Old School," in *The Vibe History of Hip-Hop*, 3.

29. Ibid., 3–10. See also Murray Forman's argument that "the evolution of hip-hop corresponds with cultural theorist Raymond Williams's observation that the process of 'formal innovation' is gradual, and while 'residual' cultural practices from prior eras continue, new 'emergent' cultural forms and practices may arise that challenge or disrupt the cultural dominant." Forman, "'Hip-Hop Ya Don't Stop': Hip-Hop History and Historiography," in *That's the Joint!*, 9.

30. George, *Hip-Hop America*, 17.

31. Jorge "Popmaster Fabel" Pabon, "Physical Graffiti: The History of Hip-Hop Dance," in *That's the Joint!*, 58.

32. "In the simplest form, a mixer will have two channels, normally with each channel split into one phono input and one line input. The input type will be switchable, normally via a toggle switch. Each channel will have its own level of control, in the form of a vertical channel facer, generally referred to as the "up" fader. This mechanism is essential in keeping the levels going to the cross fader consistent. The cross fader, where the actual mixing occurs, is near the bottom of the mixer. The cross fader is a horizontal sliding lever, which allows the DJ to affect a single record or to move easily back and forth between two turntables when working with multiple records. In hip-hop, DJs usually used two turntables, with headphones connected to a mixer." Bynoe, *Encyclopedia of Rap and Hip-Hop Culture*, 267.

33. "Sometimes the breakbeat is accompanied by other percussion instruments such as congas, timbales, bongos, or by bass guitars and saxophones, usually in a 4/4 measure. Usually the breakbeat is found either in the beginning or in the middle of the song, typically with a gradual build up, often started with horns. Rap lyricist use breakbeats to rhyme over and B-Boys use them to dance to." Bynoe, *Encyclopedia of Rap and Hip-Hop Culture*, 43.

34. Hager, *Hip-Hop*, 33. Quoted in Rose, *Black Noise*, 52.

35. Rose, *Black Noise*, 53.

36. Ibid., 51.

37. George, *Hip-Hop America*, 18.

38. Rose, *Black Noise*, 78.

39. Bynoe, *Encyclopedia of Rap and Hip-Hop Culture*, xx.

40. Craig Castleman, "The Politics of Graffiti," in *That's the Joint!*, 13–21.

41. Rose, *Black Noise*, 42.

42. George, *Hip-Hop America*, 15.

43. Rose, *Black Noise*, 85.

44. Ibid., 3.

45. Gates and McKay, eds., *The Norton Anthology of African American Literature*, 60.

46. Salaam, "The Aesthetics of Rap," 305.

47. "In essence, beatboxing is making music with the mouth. Rhythm, beats, and melody are achieved with the mouth and throat alone, simulating anything form musical instruments to turntable scratching and creating a wide range of sound effects. Some of the most popular beatboxers have been Doug E. Fresh, Biz Markie, Buffy (of the Fat Boys), and most recently Rahzel (of the Roots)." Bynoe, *Encyclopedia of Rap and Hip-Hop Culture*, 19.

48. Rose, *Black Noise*, 56.

49. Hess, *Hip-Hop in America*, xiv.

50. Rose, *Black Noise*, 56.

51. Keith Rogers (Sire Jukebox), interview with author.

52. Anthony Harris (DJ Luscious Ice), phone interview with author.

53. Eric Kaiser (K-Rino), interview with author.

54. Rose, *Black Noise*, 56.

55. Bynoe, *Encyclopedia of Rap and Hip-Hop Culture*, 273.

56. Harry Allen, "Time Bomb: Clocking the History of Hip-Hop 15 Years After 'Rapper's Delight'" *Vibe*, December 1994, 71.

57. Ibid.

58. Ibid, 72.

59. Vincent Canby, "Beat Street (1984)," *New York Times*, June 8, 1984.

60. Allen, "Time Bomb," 72.

61. George, *Hip-Hop America*, 131.

62. John Nova Lomax, "Mouth of the South: The South Park Coalition Turns 20," *Houston Press*, September 13, 2007.

63. See Benedict Anderson's definition of imagined communities and his claims of modulation in Anderson, *Imagined Communities*, 6, 163; See Partha Chatterjee's objections to Anderson's claims of modulation in Chatterjee, *The Nation and Its Fragments*, 5. Comparatively, this analysis argues that hip-hop historiography has created an imagined community of hip-hop culture. In doing so, it unintentionally claimed that everything outside of East Coast and West Coast hip-hop is simply a modulation, making only East Coast and West Coast true subjects.

64. Farley, "Hip-Hop Nation"; Forman, "'Represent'," 65.

65. See Mickey Hess's claims about how hip-hop outside of the New York City boroughs is "otherized" in dialogue and official texts. Hess, *Hip-Hop in America*, xii.

66. Sarig, *Third Coast*, xiv–xv.

67. Hess, *Hip-Hop in America*; Sarig, *Third Coast*; Westoff, *Dirty South*.

68. Mickey Hess promised to offer a text that provided the social and cultural history of each site covered, but the story on Houston does not live up to this promise. The author who reported on Houston's hip-hop culture, Jamie Lynch, failed to provide the contexts that created Houston's hip-hop culture by not talking about neighborhoods, club scenes, migration, radio stations or the development of the culture before Rap-A-Lot/Geto Boys.

69. Houston rapper Lil' Flip received an Exceptional album rating from *Vibe* magazine in 2004. Benjamin Meadows-Ingram, review of "Lil' Flip: *U Gotta Feel Me*," *Vibe*, May 2004, 160. Houston rapper Slim Thug received a Superior album rating from *Vibe* magazine in 2005. Rondell Conway, review of "Slim Thug: *Already Platinum*," *Vibe*, May 2005, 140. In a 2005 article entitled "Tipped Off," journalist Benjamin Meadows-Ingram chronicled the late twentieth-century and early twenty-first-century trajectory of success of Houston's hip-hop culture and questioned its staying power. He began the articles by noting, "While the ATL has become the capital of southern hip-hop, HOUSTON has been steadily rising. But with Mike Jones, Paul Wall, and Slim Thug on the short list of lone stars, can H-Town rap be screwed in more ways than one?" Benjamin Meadows-Ingram, "Tipped Off," *Vibe*, August 2005, 119–22. Two years later, it seems that music show director, radio host and critic Matt Sonzala questioned the same thing in his *Vibe* magazine article entitled "Still Tippin'." In this article, Sonzala traced the up-and-down successes of that same crop (plus Chamillionaire and Lil' Flip) of rappers since their major label debuts and national attention. All were spreading their musical wings and expanding their brands, intent on keeping Houston on the map. Matt Sonzala, "Still Tippin'," *Vibe*, May 2007, 92–95.

70. Lomax, "Mouth of the South: The South Park Coalition Turns 20."

71. Ibid.

72. Here, Houston and Texas fit within the southern imaginary. Houston's exclusion, or rather surface treatment, in the larger historiography of hip-hop follows the trend of other southern spaces and topics within the larger national narrative. The South is often deemed unworthy of solid interrogation, save for the typical themes and topics: slavery, Jim Crow, race, Civil Rights, etc.

CHAPTER 2

73. James Bolden, interview with Roger Wood, May 22, 1998. Quoted in Wood, *Down in Houston*, 308.

74. David Nelson, "Editorial," *Living Blues*, January/February 1997, 6. Quoted in Wood, *Down in Houston*, ix.

75. In referring to the exclusion of Houston in the rock-and-roll narrative, Roger Wood evinced that Robert Palmer cited Houston as the place where the first rock-and-roll single, "Rock Awhile" by Goree Carter and His Hepcats, was recorded in 1949. Wood said, "In making his case, Palmer debunks the now fairly widespread belief that the 1951 Chess recording (in Memphis) of "Rocket 88" by Jackie Brenston and His Delta Cats (featuring Ike Turner on piano) is the original African American progenitor of the new 'rock' sound. As John Nova Lomax has pointed out, Palmer also indirectly reminds us that, in this case as well as other instances, Houston's significant role in modern American music history has been overlooked, especially given the Delta-centric or Chicago-centric assumptions of many music writers." Wood, *Down in Houston*, 47.

76. John F. Kennedy, "Address at Rice University on the Nation's Space Effort," (lecture, Rice University, Houston, Texas, September 12, 1962). John F.

Kennedy Presidential Library and Museum, http://www.jfklibrary.org/JFK/Historic-Speeches.

77. The Houston Astros were originally named the Colt .45s. Rumor has it that after a pending lawsuit from the Colt Firearms Company, team owner Judge Roy Hofheinz met with astronauts from NASA and later settled on the name Astros (short for astronauts). The Houston Rockets were originally the San Diego Rockets, a name referencing the local rocket program at General Dynamics. The franchise was moved to Houston in 1971.

78. Chris Gray, "Lightnin' Strikes," *Houston Press*, February 10, 2010.

79. It is possible that such negations in the local history of African Americans and their music culture existed because of the biases against local and urban history. In 1992, Howard Beeth argued that "for years, most professional historians seldom assigned any real value to local studies, and they were content to leave such work to amateurs, antiquarians, and genealogies. Grass-roots history was widely regarded as history with the brains taken out." Beeth and Wintz, *Black Dixie*, 5. Another possibility for this lack of analysis is because the local academies—University of Houston, Rice University, Texas Southern University and University of St. Thomas—did not invest research into local issues until only recently.

80. Fuermann, *Houston: The Once and Future City*; Johnston, *Houston: The Unknown City*; McComb, *Houston: The Bayou City*; Shelton and Kennedy, *Houston: Supercity of the Southwest*.

81. Significant works include *A Night of Violence* (1976), "The Darker Side of 'Heaven'" (1980), *Invisible Houston* (1987), *The Red Diary* (1991) and *Black Dixie Afro-Texan History and Culture in Houston* (1992). Also notable are the following works of Dr. Merline Pitre: *Through Many Dangers, Toils, and Snares: Black Leadership in Texas* (1997), *In Struggle Against Jim Crow: Lulu B. White and the NAACP, 1900–1957* (1999) and *Black Women in Texas History* (2008). Pitre's work placed Houston and Texas into the halls of civil rights history by redressing years of discourse that had focused only on the national civil rights battles and national leaders.

82. *Historic Houston: An Illustrated History and Resource Guide* (1997), *Houston 175: A Pictorial Celebration of Houston's 175-Year History* (2011), *Cinema Houston: From Nickelodeon to Megaplex* (2007).

83. Wood, *Down in Houston*, 28.

84. Christian, "Texas Beginnings: Houston in the World of Jazz," 145.

85. There is some evidence from the oral histories conducted by Wood that whites sometimes patronized black clubs and diners, but most performances took place in segregated settings. Wood noted, "There might have been occasional visitors from the other side of the tracks. But extensive oral history confirms that those cross-cultural exchanges were the exception rather than the norm, particularly before the mid-1960s. On the other hand, many black blues musicians—the versatile Harry Hayes (b. 1924) is a prime example—also played in combos or big bands that regularly performed a wide variety of popular music styles for all-white supper-club audiences and the like. But these typically were gigs where black music culture was not so much celebrated as it was modified and assimilated to accommodate a different audience." Wood, *Down in Houston*, 30.

86. Christian, "Texas Beginnings"; Marchiafava and Stephenson, "A Feeling for Jazz," 123–43; Milton Larkin Collection, Houston Metropolitan Research Center, Houston Public Library.

87. Christian, "Texas Beginnings"; Marchiafava and Stephenson, "A Feeling for Jazz"; Arnett Cobb Collection MSS 322, Houston Metropolitan Research Center, Houston Public Library.

88. Milton Larkin Collection; Christian, "Texas Beginnings"; Arnett Cobb Collection.

89. Christian, "Texas Beginnings"; Swingmusic.net, "Illinois Jacquet," http://www. swingmusic.net/Illinois_Jacquet_Big_Band_And_Jazz_Legend_Biography.html.

90. Wood, *Down in Houston*, 113.

91. Christian, "Texas Beginnings"; Daisy Richards Collection, Houston Metropolitan Research Center, Houston Public Library.

92. Donna P. Parker, "Spivey, Victoria Regina," The Handbook of Texas Online. http://www.tshaonline.org/handbook/online/articles/fsp25.

93. Donna P. Parker, "Wallace, Beulah Thomas (Sippie)," The Handbook of Texas Online. http://www.tshaonline.org/handbook/online/articles/fwaal. According to Parker, these songs "included 'Lazy Man Blues,' penned by her brother Hersal, and her own composition, 'Special Delivery Blues,' as well as such classics as 'Mighty Tight Woman' and 'Woman Be Wise.'"

94. Ibid.

95. Wood, *Down in Houston*, x.

96. Ken Sharp, "Interview with Ringo Starr," *Record Collector*, May 2003, 84–85.

97. William Michael Smith, "Soul City: Talent Scouts Lola Anne Cullum and Lela Macy," *Houston Press*, February 24, 2011. Cullum was a middle-class African American woman who was married to a local dentist. She became interested in the blues music coming out of the Third Ward and Fifth Ward in the early 1940s, so much so that she decided to try her hand at talent scouting. Cullum is responsible for giving Smith and Hopkins their lifelong monikers: Thunder and Lightnin'.

98. Bob Ruggiero, "'Mojo Hand' Looks at Lightnin' Hopkins the Man," *Houston Chronicle*, April 17, 2013.

99. Frank Scott, "The Story of Lightnin' Hopkins," Texas Music Collection, Special Collections, University of Houston Library.

100. Chris Gray, "Lightnin' Hopkins Finally Wins a Grammy," *Houston Press*, February 7, 2013.

101. Andrew Dansby, "Robey's Place in R&B History Goes on Record Among First Blacks to Run Music Company," *Houston Chronicle*, April 16, 2011.

102. Wood, *Down in Houston*, 197.

103. Ibid.

104. Wood, *Down in Houston*, 198–99.

105. Christine M. Kreiser, "Don Robey and Duke-Peacock Records," Year of the Blues, http://www.yearoftheblues.org/features.asp?id={024252EB-DB9F-447B-B3AA-CF3CE5C231CA}&type=Feature.

106. Dansby, "Robey's Place in R&B History."

107. Wood, *Down in Houston*, 201.
108. Wilbur McFarland, interview with Roger Wood, Houston, Texas, November 3, 1997. Quoted in Wood, *Down in Houston*, 308.
109. Tara Dooley, "Creole Culture and Tradition Collide at Area Churches," *Houston Chronicle*, February 5, 2006.
110. Ibid.
111. Wood, *Down in Houston*, 48, 138–46.
112. Frazier, *Tighten Up*.
113. Archie Bell and the Drells, "Tighten Up," *Tighten Up*, Atlantic Records, 1968.
114. Archie Bell quoted in Corcoran, *All Over the Map*, 28.

Chapter 3

115. Rose, *Black Noise*, 60.
116. George, *Hip-Hop America*, 131.
117. According to Bullard, "Houston soon emerged as the premier Sunbelt city in the mid-1970s, becoming the mecca of thousands of individuals seeking new opportunities. More than five thousand persons each month migrated to 'Boomtown USA' during the city's heyday, the mid-seventies. The relatively low cost of living, the large number of new jobs created, the phenomenal housing units, combined with the potential for earning above-average income all contributed to Houston's being tagged the 'golden buckle' of the Sunbelt." Bullard, *Invisible Houston*, 7.
118. Bullard noted, "The January 1981 unemployment rate was 4.6 percent overall, 3.8 percent for whites, and nearly twice that rate—7.5 percent—for blacks. The area's unemployment rate jumped from 4.6 percent in January 1981 to 9.1 percent in January 1983. For the same time period, black unemployment increased from 7.5 percent to 15.2 percent. The unemployment gap between blacks and whites actually widened after the 1982 recession. The black unemployment rate was 2.9 percentage points higher than the white unemployment rate in January 1982 but was 6.1 percentage points higher a year later. Black were 17.2 percent of the Houston area work force but constituted more than 28.7 percent of the unemployed workers. The unemployment gap remained high through the bust period of the mid-eighties. The January 1986 unemployment rate was 5.7 percent for whites and 12.5 percent for black, a difference of nearly 7 percentage points." Bullard, *Invisible Houston*, 78–79.
119. Ibid., 8.
120. Ibid., 10.
121. Wicked Cricket, panel discussion at H.E.R.E. Project Legacy Awards, March 23, 2010.
122. Lance Scott Walker, "SPC Weekend Plumbs the Roots of Houston Rap," *Houston Press*, September 11, 2008.
123. James Smith, now known as James Prince, began Rap-A-Lot Records in 1986 and was responsible for the careers of the Geto Boys. Russell Washington began Big Tyme Records in the late 1980s and was initially responsible for the early

success of UGK. Troy Birklett, better known as Lil' Troy, began Short Stop Records in 1988 and was the first to sign Brad Jordan (DJ Akshen/Scarface) to a record deal.

124. Carlos Garza (DJ Styles), interview with author.

125. Anthony Harris (DJ Luscious Ice), phone interview with author.

126. Cap rapping is hip-hop's version of "the dozens." *The Norton Anthology of African American Literature* notes, "It derives from playground, pool hall, barber shop, and beauty salon narration and argumentation and from the highly competitive boasts and toasts (like 'The Signifyin' Monkey') and from the dozens (an age-old verbal dance of derision in which one trades insults with one's opponent while trying to stay cool under the pressure of hearing oneself potentially outwitted by ribald verbal darts aimed at one's closets family members [or one's personal "defects"]). Gates et al., *The Norton Anthology of African American Literature*, 78.

127. In discussing the early development of graffiti culture within hip-hop culture, George remarked, "Yet there is a youthful integrity and humor to them that reminds us in the jaded '90s that hip-hop didn't start as a career move but as a way of announcing one's existence to the world." George, *Hip-Hop America*, 14.

128. Keith Rogers (Sire Jukebox), interview with author.

129. Similar to a game of the dozens, a battle rap is an improvised rap performed in competition with another rapper or rappers to earn bragging rights as a great lyricist. Battle raps were typically performed in cafeterias or on playgrounds and street corners or any other place where budding rappers and a crowd could congregate for a competition. Battle raps are performed a cappella or with a beat provided by a beatboxer or any percussive object. See also Bynoe, *Encyclopedia of Rap and Hip-Hop Culture*, 15.

130. "To freestyle is to create rhymes on the spot—spontaneously and contemporaneously—as opposed to memorizing or reciting previously written works." Bynoe, *Encyclopedia of Rap and Hip-Hop Culture*, 141.

131. Eric Kaiser (K-Rino), interview with author.

132. Willie Dennis (Willie D), phone interview with author.

133. Eric Kaiser (K-Rino), panel discussion at H.E.R.E. Project Legacy Awards, March 23, 2010.

134. Oscar Ceres (Raheem), phone interview with author.

135. Ibid.

136. William Ross (Def Jam Blaster), interview with author.

137. Bynoe, *Encyclopedia of Rap and Hip-Hop Culture*, 70.

138. Anthony Harris (DJ Luscious Ice), phone interview with author.

139. Ibid.

140. Nelson George, "Nationwide: America Raps Back," *Village Voice*, 1988.

141. Ibid.

142. In a 1991 article in the *Houston Chronicle*, Michael Meyer paraphrased and quoted Steve Fournier: "'Indeed, Houston is the second-largest seller of rap music and concerts,' said Steve Fournier, a rap-music distributor and disc jockey at Club Infinity. 'No other city plays as much rap on the radio.'" Michael Meyer, "Rap Attention/Hip-Hop Gear Goes High Fashion," *Houston Chronicle*, June 13, 1991.

143. Guy Bouldin, "Houston Night Club Mogul Legend Ray Burnett Dies at Age 81," Taylors of Houston E-News Letter, January 16, 2012. http://www.taylorsofhouston.com/e-news11612.htm.

144. Lee Audrey Roberts (Trudy Lynn) quoted in Govenar, *Texas Blues*, 326.

145. George, "Nationwide."

146. Steve Fournier, interview with author.

147. A "club head" is a person who attends nightclubs on a frequent basis.

148. Steve Fournier, interview with author.

149. Ibid.

150. Ibid.

151. Fournier recalled, "When I first heard rap, something in my mind clicked. Something told me, 'This is your thing.' I don't want to compare it to a religious experience, but it was almost like getting saved." Steve Fournier quoted in Rick Mitchell, "Rap Zooms to No.1 on the Charts" *Houston Chronicle*, January 20, 1991.

152. Fournier, interview with author.

153. Ibid.

154. Keith Rogers (Sire Jukebox), interview with author.

155. George, "Nationwide." Gilley's was a huge bar/nightclub/honky-tonk located in Pasadena, Texas, that opened in 1917. It was owned by country music singer Mickey Gilley and businessman Sherwood Cryer. In 1980, Gilley's was the muse and central filming location for the movie *Urban Cowboy*, starring John Travolta.

156. Roni Sarig noted that Vanilla Ice "made regular trips to Houston, where he rocked the weekly competitions at the Rhinestone Wrangler [and] was a frequent combatant of Willie Dennis (aka future Geto Boy Willie D)." Sarig, *Third Coast*, 44.

157. Steve Fournier, interview with author.

158. Willie D quoted in Sarig, *Third Coast*, 44.

159. Ibid, 44–45.

160. Ibid., 37.

161. Cobb reasoned, "But what made the era they inaugurated worthy of the term *golden*—an adjective gleaned from that longest glorified of precious metals in hip-hop—was the sheer number of stylistic innovations that came into existence. The era witnessed the emergence of definitive influences Big Daddy Kane, Queen Latifah, Ice Cube, the Ultra Magnetic MCs, Main Source, 2 Live Crew, Cypress Hill, L.L. Cool J, MC Lyte, Slick Rick, Too Short, KRS-One, Doug E. Fresh, EPMD, Kool G. Rap, Ice-T, Biz-Markie, NWA, Rakim—almost all of whom were under twenty-one years of age when they made their debuts." Cobb, *To the Break of Dawn*, 47.

162. Lester "Sir" Pace, phone interview with author.

163. Eric Kaiser (K-Rino), interview with author.

164. Lester "Sir" Pace, phone interview with author.

165. Jennifer Montgomery, "In Tune with Its Customers/Soundwaves' Success Formula: Give Listeners What They Want," *Houston Chronicle*, March 29, 2000.

166. Carlos Garza (DJ Styles), interview with author.

167. Terry Hayes quoted in Jennifer Montgomery, "In Tune with Its Customers/Soundwaves' Success Formula."

168. Carlos Garza (DJ Styles), interview with author.
169. Ibid.
170. Mitchell, "Rap Zooms to No. 1."

CHAPTER 4

171. Steve Fournier quoted in George, "Nationwide."
172. Bernard Freeman (Bun B), "Country Cousins."
173. L.A. Rapper, "MacGregor Park," SDR Records, 1985; Real Chill, "Rockin' It," Boom-Town Stars, 1986; Ghetto Boys, "Car Freaks," Rap-A-Lot Records, 1986.
174. Parking-lot pimping means showing off the features of your car, especially rims and a sound system, with the aim of attracting the attention of a woman or respect from other guys.
175. Anthony Harris (DJ Luscious Ice), phone interview with author.
176. Electro-hop (aka electro or electro funk) is "a type of dance music combined with rap music that emerged in southern California in the early 1980s. The subgenre of rap music (also known simply as electro) was popularized by rap artists such as World Class Wreckin' Cru, The Egyptian Lover, and The Arabian Prince. Electro-hop was the prevailing from of West Coast rap during this period; however, many East Coast critics and rap music purists disliked electro-hop and considered it as a bastardized form of rap music." Bynoe, *Encyclopedia of Rap and Hip-Hop Culture*, 116.
177. See Jamie Lynch's discussion on Houston's car culture and its role in Houston hip-hop in "The Long, Hot Grind: How Houston Engineered an Industry of Independence," in Hess, *Hip-Hop in America*, 445; See Murray Forman's explication about "homeboys and production posses" in Forman, "'Represent',"71; On the final verse of "MacGregor Park," the L.A. Rapper recommended that you must bring a "yellow hammer" with you the next time you come to the park. A yellow hammer is an old colloquialism to describe a lighter or fair-skinned black woman. Based on hegemonic influences, a yellow hammer was considered the standard of beauty for a black woman. Mentions of a yellow hammer, yellow bone or yella' continued to dominate the lyrical content of Houston rap music in the late 1990s and early 2000s.
178. To "rock a mic" means to show great verbal dexterity through style and flow.
179. Walker, "SPC Weekend Plumbs the Roots of Houston Rap."
180. James Smith began using the name James Prince about 1990. Within this analysis, James Smith will be used until the point where he begins to use the name James Prince.
181. Carolyn Chambers Sanders and Al Brown, "James Prince Directs Rap-A-Lot Records to Profits and Respectability," *Link Magazine*, April 1999, 14–15, 18–20.
182. James Smith was quoted as saying, "Well, I grew up where poverty was a serious burden on my family, and that had a major part in my mind developing. I wanted to break that poverty curse that existed. Even as a kid, I was somewhat abnormal for my age when it came to trying to have a dollar. I was seven or eight years old, and a lot of [other kids] were thinking about playing, but I was

thinking about how to get a dollar, whether it was through cutting yards or whatever it may have been." Andrew Noz, "'It Was Like Flies to Honey': 25 Years of Rap-A-Lot Records," NPR, February 10, 2012. http://www.npr.org/blogs/therecord/2012/01/23/143799814/it-was-like-flies-to-honey-25-years-of-rap-a-lot-records.

183. *Ring Magazine*, March 2000, 42.

184. Clyde Smith, "Yung Ro Completes Freshman Video For 'Donk Dat Remix,'" *HipHop Press*, April 24, 2009. http://www.hiphoppress.com/2009/04/yung-ro-completes-freshman-video-for-donk-dat-remix.

185. Sarig, *Third Coast*, 41.

186. Thelton Polk (K9/Sir Rap-A-Lot), letter to author.

187. Oscar Ceres (Raheem), phone interview with author.

188. Keith Rogers (Sire Jukebox), interview with author.

189. Ibid.

190. Ibid.

191. Oscar Ceres (Raheem), phone interview with author.

192. Keith Rogers (Sire Jukebox), interview with author.

193. Ibid.

194. Miguel Burke, "Enemy of the State," *The Source*, April 2003, 100.

195. Noz, "'It Was Like Flies to Honey.'"

196. Captain Jack, "Sexy Girls," Rap-A-Lot Records, 1987.

197. "The Sexiest But Worst Rap-A-Lot Record," Cocaine Blunts, http://www.cocaineblunts.com/blunts/?p=6109.

198. Oscar Ceres (Raheem), phone interview with author.

199. Ibid. Ceres said, "'Car Freaks' was something that J [James Prince] created. See, that's when the commercialization of hip-hop really started. Had it been up to me and Jukebox and K9, for that matter, the song probably would not have been 'Car Freaks.' [It] was more or less J's brainchild, and that was the beginning of the end of artists' creative freedom…at Rap-A-Lot Records. And that's why I wanted to leave the Ghetto Boys, not because I didn't wanna be with my squad, but it was like he was telling us what to say and what to write. That was something that me and Box—we wasn't used to that shit. We was used to writing what the hell we wanted to write. And now, here is somebody telling us what he wants us to write, and that became a problem for me."

200. Ibid.

201. Dynasty Williams, "DJ Ready Red: The Original Geto Boy," AllHipHop.com, May 20, 2008. http://allhiphop.com/2008/05/20/dj-ready-red-the-ultimate-transforming-the-original-geto-boy/.

202. Collins Leysath (DJ Ready Red), phone interview with author.

203. Ibid.

204. Ricardo Royal (Gangsta Ric), interview with author.

205. Ibid.

206. Ibid.

207. Sarig, *Third Coast*, 42.

208. Ibid, 43.

209. A hype man is "an individual whose job is to highlight the MC during live performances by pumping up the audience and demanding that people listen to the MC's lyrics." Bynoe, *Encyclopedia of Rap and Hip-Hop Culture*, 176.

210. Richard Baimbridge, "The Enchanted Forest: Carl Stephenson on Beck, the Geto Boys, Trip-Hop, and the Fine Line between Dream and Reality," *Dallas Observer*, January 29, 1998.

211. Ghetto Boys, *Making Trouble*, Rap-A-Lot Records, 1988; Royal Flush, *Uh Oh!*, Rap-A-Lot Records, 1988; Def IV, *Nice and Hard*, Rap-A-Lot Records, 1988; Raheem, *The Vigilante*, A&M Records, 1988.

212. Lynch, "The Long, Hot Grind," in Hess, *Hip-Hop in America*, 430.

213. Oscar Ceres (Raheem), phone interview with author.

214. Raheem, "5th Ward," *The Vigilante*, A&M Records, 1988.

215. Oscar Ceres (Raheem), phone interview with author.

216. Ibid.

217. Dennis Hunt, "No Hick Jokes, Please," *Los Angeles Times*, October 29, 1988.

218. Ibid.

219. Sarig, *Third Coast*, 43.

220. Ibid.

221. Ibid.

222. Collins Leysath (DJ Ready Red), phone interview with author.

223. Ibid.

224. "Meet the Ghetto Boys," *Right On*, 1988, 52.

225. Ricardo Royal (Gangsta Ric), interview with author.

226. Ibid.

227. Maco L. Faniel, "UGK," in Jasinski, ed., *The Handbook of Texas Music*, 638–39.

228. Sarig, *Third Coast*, 55.

229. Ghetto Boys, *Be Down*, Rap-A-Lot Records, 1988.

230. Keith Rogers (Sire Jukebox), interview with author.

231. Noz, "'It Was Like Flies to Honey.'"

232. Willie Dennis (Willie D), phone interview with author.

233. Ibid.

234. Sarig, *Third Coast*, 45.

235. Ibid.

236. William Ross (Def Jam Blaster), interview with author.

237. Ibid.

238. Troy Birklet (Lil' Troy), interview with author.

239. DJ Akshen/Scarface, *Scarface*, Short Stop Records, 1989.

240. The Soul Searchers, "Ashley's Roachclip," *Salt of the Earth*, Sussex Records, 1974; Le Pamplemousse, "Gimmie What You Got," AVI Records, 1976.

241. Sarig, *Third Coast*, 45.

242. Westoff, *Dirty South*, 47.

243. Burke, "Enemy of the State"; Thelton Polk (K9/Sir Rap-A-Lot), letter to author.

244. Keith Rogers (Sire Jukebox), interview with author.

245. Sarig, *Third Coast*, 46.

246. Willie Dennis (Willie D), phone interview with author; Sarig, *Third Coast*, 47; Ghetto Boys, "Size Ain't Shit," *Grip It! On That Other Level*, Rap-A-Lot Records, 1989.

247. Matthias Jost, "Willie D: Controversy," RapReviews.com, http://www.rapreviews.com/archive/BTTL_controversy.html.

248. See Roni Sarig's review of the album in Sarig, *Third Coast*, 47–49.

249. See Prince's claim about record sales in Noz, "'It Was Like Flies to Honey.'"

250. Bynoe noted, "Def Jam Recordings stands out as the record label most influential of rap music. Through its charismatic leader, Russell Simmons, Def Jam Recordings for nearly two decades defined the look and sound of the genre. It was instrumental also in branding hip-hop for worldwide consumption. The origin of Def Jam Recordings' empire dates to when rap music promoter Russell Simmons met Rick Rubin, a New York University student. Simmons and Rubin shared a love of raw and street-wise rap music and became business partners." Bynoe, *Encyclopedia of Rap and Hip-Hop Culture*, 82–83.

251. Collins Leysath (DJ Ready Red), phone interview with author.

252. Jon Pareles, "Distributor Withdraws Rap Album Over Lyrics," *New York Times*, August 28, 1990.

253. Charnas, *The Big Payback*, 360–62.

254. Alan Light, "Gangster Summit Falters," *Rolling Stone*, February 7, 1991, 28.

255. R.A. Dyer and Rick Mitchell, "Geto Boys' Music Blamed in a Slaying in Dodge City," *Houston Chronicle*, July 23, 1991.

256. Ibid.

257. Barbara Jaeger, "Those Who Would Have Us Hear No Evil," *The Record*, June 26, 1992.

258. Charnas, *The Big Payback*, 361–62.

259. Willie Dennis (Willie D), phone interview with author.

260. Choice, *The Big Payback*, Rap-A-Lot Records, 1990.

261. Convicts, *Convicts*, Rap-A-Lot Records, 1991.

262. Westoff, *Dirty South*, 51–52.

263. O.G. Style, *I Know How to Play 'Em*, Rap-A-Lot Records, 1991.

264. Robbie Ettelson, "DJ Vicious Lee (Def IV) Interview," Unkut.com, http://www.unkut.com/2008/06/dj-vicious-lee-def-iv-interview/.

265. Jazzie Redd, "I Am A Dope Fiend," *Spice of Life*, Pump Records, 1990.

266. Jazzie Redd, *Top Secret*, Redd Smoke Records, 1987.

267. Jazzie Redd (Rodney Edmonson Sr.), phone interview with author.

268. King Tee, *Act a Fool*, Capitol Records, 1988.

269. Jazzie Redd, *Beach Girl*, Pump Records, 1990.

270. Jazzie Redd (Rodney Edmonson Sr.), phone interview with author.

271. Thelton Polk (K9/Sir Rap-A-Lot), letter to author.

272. Keith Rogers (Sire Jukebox), interview with author.

273. Collins Leysath (DJ Ready Red), phone interview with author.

274. David Mills, "The Geto Boys, Beating the Murder Rap: How Did Blood and Guts Get from the Streets to Top 40?" *Washington Post*, December 15, 1991.

275. Anthony DeCurtis, "Geto Boy Bushwick Bill Shot in Head," *Rolling Stone*, June 27, 1991, 17.

276. See Sarig's review in Sarig, *Third Coast*, 51.

277. Coleman, *Check the Technique*, 226.

278. Geto Boys, *We Can't Be Stopped*, Rap-A-Lot Records, 1991.

279. Coleman, *Check the Technique*, 226.

280. Ibid.

281. Noz, "'It Was Like Flies to Honey.'"

282. Collins Leysath (DJ Ready Red), phone interview with author.

283. Geto Boys, "Mind Playing Tricks on Me," *We Can't Be Stopped*, Rap-A-Lot Records, 1991.

284. Isaac Hayes, "Hung Up on My Baby," *Tough Guys*, Stax, 1974; Biz Markie, "Pickin' Boogers," *Goin' Off*, Cold Chillin, 1988.

285. See Sarig's review of the album Sarig, *Third Coast*, 52.

286. Scarface, *Mr. Scarface Is Back*, Rap-A-Lot Records, 1991.

287. Reef, "Music Review: *Mr. Scarface Is Back*," *The Source*, December 1991.

Afterword

288. Much of the background information on DJ Screw's music comes from conversations the author has had with members of his family and a number of his friends between 2010 and 2013.

289. Lil' Keke, panel discussion at Awready!: The Houston Hip-Hop Conference, March 28, 2012.

290. These included Lil' Keke, *Don't Mess wit Texas* (Jam Down Records, 1997); *Ghetto Dreams* (Wreckshop Records, 1998); Big Pokey, *Hardest Pit in the Litter* (Chevis Entertainment, 1999); Yungstar, *Throwed Yung Playa* (Straight Profit, 2000); Big Moe, *City of Syrup* (Wreckshop Records, 2000); HAWK, *Under HAWK's Wings* (Dead End Records, 2000); Lil' Flip, *The Leprechaun* (Sucka Free, 2000); and Lil' O, *Da Fat Rat wit da Cheez* (Game Face Records, 2001).

291. *Houston Chronicle*, "Local Rapper Shot to Death As He Went to Collect for Show," February 4, 1998.

292. Allan Turner, "Producer May Have OD'd, Police Say," *Houston Chronicle*, November 18, 2000; *Houston Chronicle*, "Record Producer's Death Caused by Drug Overdose," January 9, 2001. Note: Date of death may be correctly inferred as November 16, 2000, in the November 18, 2000 article but is incorrect in the January 9, 2001 article.

293. Michael D. Clark, "Few Clues in Killing of Houston Rapper," *Houston Chronicle*, May 3, 2006; Eyder Peralta, "Kenneth 'Big Moe' Moore, 1974–2007," *Houston Chronicle*, October 16, 2007; *New York Times*, "Drugs Killed Pimp C," February 6, 2008.

294. *BEEF IV*, "Houston: Northside vs. Southside," https://www.youtube.com/watch?v=C2DiQwwaPYo.

295. "Tippin'" refers to lowering one side of a car using hydraulics, "fours" (also called "'84s") are spoked rims made by Cadillac in 1984 and "vogues" are whitewall tires with gold trim.

296. The song was "Sittin' Sidewayz," featuring Big Pokey.

297. Joseph Patel and Sway Callaway, "Chopped and Screwed: A History," MTV News, 2005. http://www.mtv.com/bands/h/hip_hop_week/chopped_screwed/index3.jhtml.

298. Interview with Chamillionaire following the 2007 Grammy Awards, February 11, 2007. http://www.youtube.com/watch?v=Nk7um99zZcU.

299. AllMusic.com, "Scarface," http://www.allmusic.com/artist/scarface-mn0000315463.

300. Scarface, "I Never Seen a Man Die," *The Diary*, Rap-A-Lot Records, 1994.

301. David Kaplan, "Houston Music Distributor Fights to Stay in Business," Knight Ridder/Tribune Business News, February 5, 2003.

302. K-Rino, from *Houston Rap* panel discussion held at the Houston Museum of African American Culture, April 20, 2013.

303. K-Rino, "Raised in the Dead End," *Book Number 7*, Black Book International, 2007.

304. Timothy Bella, "Should Hip-Hop Artists Be Allowed to Release Albums From Jail?" *The Atlantic*, August 29, 2012.

305. Ibid.

306. AllMusic.com, "Baby Bash," http://www.allmusic.com/artist/baby-bash-mn0000069813.

307. Rolando Rodriguez, "Up on His Hustle," *Houston Press*, January 6, 2010.

308. Joey Guerra, "Chingo Bling Signs on with National Distributor," *Houston Chronicle*, July 8, 2006.

309. Sarig, *Third Coast*, 55.

310. Bun B, panel discussion at Awready!: The Houston Hip-Hop Conference, March 28, 2012.

311. Ibid.

312. *Houston Chronicle*, "Million-selling Rap Star Pimp C Granted Parole—Part of Acclaimed Underground Kingz Leaves a Texas Prison After Serving Half of His Term for Assault," December 31, 2005.

313. *XXL*, "Devin the Dude Leaves Rap-A-Lot Records," February 5, 2008, http://www.xxlmag.com/xxl-magazine/2008/02/devin-the-dude-leaves-rap-a-lot-records/; Paul Meara, "Z-Ro Asked About Leaving Rap-A-Lot Records, Confirms More Mya Collaborations," HipHopDX, December 31, 2012, http://www.hiphopdx.com/index/news/id.22385/title.z-ro-asked-about-leaving-rap-a-lot-records-confirms-more-mya-collaborations; Benjamin Meadows-Ingram, "Hustlin'," *Billboard*, March 10, 2012.

314. University of Houston, "UH at a Glance," http://www.uh.edu/about/uh-glance.

315. Additional materials were donated by Nikki Williams, Andrew Hatton (DJ Chill) and Demetrius Sherman (Big Demo).

316. The donors for these materials were HAWK's wife, Meshah Hawkins; former Pen & Pixel co-owner Shawn Brauch; and Kendall Mosley. Some materials were acquired with the assistance of founding partner SoSouth.

317. The H.E.R.E. Project is now known as the Center for Engaged Research and Collaborative Learning (CERCL) and is part of the Kinder Institute for Urban Research at Rice University. In 2011, H.E.R.E. Project founder Dr. Anthony Pinn brought Bun B to campus as a distinguished visiting lecturer in religious studies. In 2012, the renamed CERCL acquired the archives of the Swishahouse label.

318. The author would like to thank Thomas Molinar Jr. and Matt Sonzala for their helpful readings of this essay (the afterword).

BIBLIOGRAPHY

PRIMARY SOURCES

Oral Histories and Personal Correspondence

Al-Amin, Rashad. Interview with author, Houston, Texas, April 10, 2011.

Birklett, Troy (Lil' Troy). Interview with author, Houston, Texas, February 1, 2012.

Ceres, Oscar (Raheem). Phone interview with author, Houston, Texas, April 30, 2011.

Collins, Pam. Interview with author, Houston, Texas, March 15, 2012.

Dennis, Willie (Willie D). Phone interview with author, Houston, Texas, February 10, 2012.

Edmonson, Rodney (Jazzie Redd). Phone interview with author, Houston, Texas, April 19, 2013.

Fournier, Steve. Interview with author, Houston, Texas, February 28, 2012.

Garza, Carlos (DJ Styles). Interview with author, Houston, Texas, January 26, 2012.

Harris, Anthony (DJ Luscious Ice). Phone interview with author, Houston, Texas, April 6, 2011.

Kaiser, Eric (K-Rino). Interview with author, Houston, Texas, April 9, 2011.

Leysath, Collins (DJ Ready Red). Phone interview with author, Houston, Texas, March 27, 2011.

Pace, Lester "Sir." Phone interview with author, Houston, Texas, March 11, 2012.

Parker, Devonn (Wicked Cricket). Interview with author, Houston, Texas, March 28, 2012.

Polk, Thelton (K9/Sir Rap-A-Lot). Letter to author, Houston, Texas, February 23, 2012.

Rogers, Keith (Sire Jukebox). Interview with author, Houston, Texas, April 5, 2011.
———. Interview with author, Houston, Texas, August 3, 2011.

Ross, William (Def Jam Blaster). Interview with author, Houston, Texas, April 4, 2011.
Royal, Rick. Interview with author, Houston, Texas, March 28, 2012.
Westoff, Ben. Interview with author, Houston, Texas, April 30, 2011.

Music Recordings

Captain Jack. *Jack it Up*. Grand Records, GR-1003, 1984.
_____. *Sexy Girls*. Rap-A-Lot Records, RAP-778, 1987.
Choice. *The Big Payback*. Rap-A-Lot Records, RAP-105-2, 1990.
Convicts. *Convicts*. Rap-A-Lot Records, SL 57152, 1991.
Def IV. *Nice and Hard*. Rap-A-Lot Records, RAP-102-1, 1988.
DJ Akshen. *Scarface*. Short Stop Records, SS 100, 1989.
Geto Boys. *The Geto Boys*. Def American Recordings, DEF 24306, 1990.
_____. *We Can't Be Stopped*. Rap-A-Lot Records, CDL 57161, 1991.
Ghetto Boys. *Be Down*. Rap-A-Lot Records, RAP-50, 1988.
_____. *Car Freaks*. Rap-A-Lot Records, RAP-777, 1986.
_____. *Grip It! On That Other Level*. Rap-A-Lot Records, RAP-103-2, 1989.
_____. *Making Trouble*. Rap-A-Lot Records, RAP-100, 1988.
Jazzie Redd. *Beach Girl*. Pump Records, VL-15130, 1990.
———. *I Am a Dope Fiend*. Spice of Life, Pump Records, CDL 15142-2, 1990.
———. *Top Secret*. Redd Smoke Records, LH-25141, 1987.
L.A. Rapper. *MacGregor Park*. SDR Records, 1985.
O.G. Style. *I Know How to Play 'Em*. Rap-A-Lot Records, CDL-57151, 1991.
Raheem. *Self Preservation*. Rap-A-Lot Records, RAP-CD17757, 1989.
———. *The Vigilante*. A&M Records, AMA 5212, 1989.
Real Chill. *Rockin' It*. Boom-Town Stars, BO-1000, 1986.
Royal Flush. *Uh Oh!* Rap-A-Lot Records, RAP-101-2, 1988.
Scarface. *Mr. Scarface Is Back*. Rap-A-Lot Records, CDL 57167, 1991.
Talib Kweli. "Country Cousins." Performed by Talib Kweli, UGK (Bun B and Pimp C) and Raheem DeVaughn, Blacksmith Music 315644-1, Warner Bros Records, 9362 49914-8, 2007.
Willie D. *Controversy*. Rap-A-Lot Records, RAP-104-4, 1989.

Books

Frazier, Skipper Lee. *Tighten Up: The Autobiography of a Houston Disc Jockey*. Houston, TX: Trafford Publishing, 2001.

Archives

Houston Hip-Hop Collection. Special Collections, University of Houston Libraries.
Texas Jazz Archives. Houston Public Library.
Texas Music Collection. Special Collections, University of Houston Libraries.

SECONDARY SOURCES

Books and Dissertations

Anderson, Benedict. *Imagined Communities: Reflections on the Origin and Spread of Nationalism*. London: Verso Books, 1991.

Asante, M.K. *It's Bigger Than Hip-Hop: The Rise of the Post-Hip-Hop Generation*. New York: St. Martin's Press, 2008.

Beeth, Howard, and Cary D. Wintz, eds. *Black Dixie: Afro-Texan History and Culture in Houston*. College Station: Texas A&M University Press, 1992.

Bell, Daniel. *The Coming of Post-Industrial Society: A Venture in Social Forecasting*. New York: Basic Books, 1973.

Bradley, Andy, and Roger Wood. *House of Hits: The Story of Houston's Gold Star/ SugarHill Recording Studios*. Austin: University of Texas Press, 2010.

Bullard, Robert D. *Invisible Houston: The Black Experience in Boom and Bust*. College Station: Texas A&M University Press, 1987.

Bynoe, Yvonne. *Encyclopedia of Rap and Hip-Hop Culture*. Westport, CT: Greenwood Press, 2006.

Cepeda, Raquel, ed. *And It Don't Stop: The Best American Hip-Hop Journalism of the Last 25 Years*. New York: Faber & Faber, 2004.

Chang, Jeff. *Can't Stop, Won't Stop: A History of the Hip-Hop Generation*. New York: St. Martin's Press, 2005.

Chapman, Betty Trapp. *Historic Houston: An Illustrated History and Resource Guide*. San Antonio, TX: Ron Lammert, 1997.

Charnas, Dan. *The Big Payback: The History of the Business of Hip-Hop*. New York: New American Library, 2010.

Chatterjee, Partha. *The Nation and Its Fragments: Colonial and Postcolonial Histories*. Princeton, NJ: Princeton University Press, 1993.

Cobb, William Jelani. *To the Break of Dawn: A Freestyle on the Hip-Hop Aesthetic*. New York: New York University Press, 2007.

Coleman, Brian. *Check the Technique: Liner Notes For Hip-Hop Junkies*. New York: Villard, 2007.

Corcoran, Michael. *All Over the Map: True Heroes of Texas Music*. Austin: University of Texas Press, 2005.

Dyson, Michael Eric. *Why I Love Black Women*. New York: Basic Civitas Books, 2003.

Ervin, Hazel Arnett. *African American Literary Criticism, 1773 to 2000*. New York: Twayne Publishers, 1999.

Forman, Murray. *The Hood Comes First: Race, Space, and Place in Rap and Hip-Hop*. Middletown: Wesleyan University Press, 2002.

Forman, Murray, and Mark Anthony Neal, eds. *That's the Joint!: The Hip-Hop Studies Reader*. 2nd ed. New York: Routledge, 2012.

Fricke, Jim, and Charlie Ahearn. *Yes Yes Y'all: The Experience Music Project Oral History of Hip-Hop's First Decade*. Cambridge, MA: Da Capo Press, 2002.

Fuermann, George. *Houston: The Once and Future City*. Garden City, NY: Doubleday, 1971.

Bibliography

Gates, Henry Louis, Jr., and Nellie Y. McKay, eds. *The Norton Anthology of African American Literature*. 2nd ed. New York: W.W. Norton & Company, 2004.

George, Nelson. *The Death of Rhythm and Blues*. New York: Pantheon Books, 1988.

————. *Hip-Hop America*. 2nd ed. New York: Penguin Books, 2005.

Glasrud, Bruce A., and Merline Pitre, eds. *Black Women in Texas History*. College Station: Texas A&M University Press, 2008.

Govenar, Alan. *Texas Blues: The Rise of a Contemporary Sound*. College Station: Texas A&M University Press, 2008.

Hager, Steven. *Hip-Hop: The Illustrated History of Break Dancing, Rap Music, and Graffiti*. New York: St Martin's Press, 1984.

Haynes, Robert V. *A Night of Violence: The Houston Riot of 1917*. Baton Rouge: Louisiana State University Press, 1976.

Hess, Mickey. *Is Hip-Hop Dead?: The Past, Present, and Future of America's Most Wanted Music*. Westport, CT: Praeger, 2007.

Hess, Mickey, ed. *Hip-Hop in America: A Regional Guide*. Santa Barbara, CA: Greenwood, 2010.

Hine, Darlene Clark, ed. *The State of Afro-American History: Past, Present, and Future*. Baton Rouge: Louisiana State University Press, 1986.

Houston Chronicle. *Houston 175*. Battle Ground, WA: Pediment Publishing, 2011.

Jasinski, Laurie E., ed. *The Handbook of Texas Music*. 2nd ed. Denton: Texas State Historical Association, 2012.

Jay-Z. *Decoded*. New York: Spiegel & Grau, 2010.

Johnston, Marguerite. *Houston: The Unknown City, 1836–1946*. College Station: Texas A&M University Press, 1991.

Jones, Howard. *The Red Diary: A Chronological History of Black Americans in Houston and Some Neighboring Harris County Communities—122 Years Later*. Austin, TX: Nortex Press, 1991.

Jones, LeRoi. *Blues People: Negro Music in White America*. New York: W. Morrow, 1967.

Kelley, Robin D.G. *Into the Fire: African Americans Since 1970*. New York: Oxford University Press, 1996.

Kelley, Robin D.G., and Earl Lewis, eds. *Race Rebels: Culture, Politics, and the Black Working Class*. New York: Free Press, 1996.

————. *To Make Our World Anew: A History of African Americans*. New York: Oxford University Press, USA, 2000.

Light, Alan, ed. *The Vibe History of Hip Hop*. New York: Three Rivers Press, 1999.

McComb, David G. *Houston: The Bayou City*. Austin: University of Texas Press, 1960.

Neal, Mark Anthony. *Soul Babies: Black Popular Culture and the Post-Soul Aesthetic*. New York: Routledge, 2002.

————. *What the Music Said: Black Popular Music and Black Public Culture*. New York: Routledge, 1999.

Ogg, Alex, and David Upshal. *The Hip-Hop Years: A History of Rap*. New York: Fromm International, 2001.

Pattillo, Mary. *Black on the Block: The Politics of Race and Class in the City*. Chicago: University of Chicago Press, 2007.

Perkins, William. *Droppin' Science: Critical Essays on Rap Music and Hip-Hop Culture*. Edited by William Eric Perkins. Philadelphia: Temple University Press, 1996.

Perry, Imani. *Prophets of the Hood: Politics and Poetics in Hip-Hop*. Durham: Duke University Press, 2004.

Pinn, Anthony B., ed. *Noise and Spirit: The Religious and Spiritual Sensibilities of Rap Music*. New York: New York University Press, 2003.

Pitre, Merline. *In Struggle Against Jim Crow: Lulu B. White and the NAACP, 1900–1957*. College Station: Texas A&M University Press, 1999.

———. *Through Many Dangers, Toils, and Snares: The Black Leadership of Texas, 1868–1900*. 2nd ed. Austin, TX: Eakin Press, 1997.

Rose, Tricia. *Black Noise: Rap Music and Black Culture in Contemporary America*. Hanover, NH: Wesleyan University Press, 1994.

———. *The Hip-Hop Wars: What We Talk About When We Talk About Hip Hop and Why It Matters*. New York: Basic Civitas Books, 2008.

Sarig, Roni. *Third Coast: OutKast, Timbaland, and How Hip-Hop Became a Southern Thing*. Cambridge, MA: Da Capo Press, 2007.

Shelton, William, and Ann Kennedy. Houston: *Supercity of the Southwest*. Garden City, NY: Dolphin Books, 1978.

Sorelle, James M. "The Darker Side of 'Heaven': The Black Community in Houston, Texas, 1917–1945." PhD dissertation, Kent State University, 1980.

Stoute, Steve, and Mim Eichler Rivas. *The Tanning of America: How Hip-Hop Created a Culture That Rewrote the Rules of the New Economy*. New York: Gotham, 2011.

Toop, David. *Rap Attack 3: African Rap to Global Hip-Hop*. 3rd rev., expanded, and updated ed. London: Serpent's Tail, 2000.

Vico, Giambattista. *New Science: Principles of the New Science Concerning the Common Nature of Nations*. 3rd ed. London: Penguin Classics, 2000.

Weissman, Dick. *Talkin' 'Bout a Revolution: Music and Social Change in America*. New York: Backbeat Books, 2010.

Welling, David. *Cinema Houston: From Nickelodeon to Megaplex*. Austin: University of Texas Press, 2007.

Westhoff, Ben. *Dirty South: Outkast, Lil' Wayne, Soulja Boy, and the Southern Rappers Who Reinvented Hip-Hop*. Chicago: Chicago Review Press, 2011.

Wood, Roger. *Down in Houston: Bayou City Blues*. Austin: University of Texas Press, 2003.

———. *Texas Zydeco*. Austin: University of Texas Press, 2006.

X, Malcolm. *Malcolm X on Afro-American History*. New York: Pathfinder Press, 1988.

Journals

Alridge, Derrick P., and James B. Steward. "Introduction Past, Present, and Future: Hip Hop in History." *Journal of African American History* 90, no. 3 (Summer 2005): 190–95.

Christian, Garna L. "Texas Beginnings: Houston in the World of Jazz." *The Houston Review: History and Culture of The Gulf Coast 12*, no. 3 (1990): 144–55.

Dagbovie, Pero Gaglo. "'Of All Our Studies, History Is the Best Qualified to Reward Our Research': Black History's Relevance to the Hip-Hop Generation." *The Journal of African American History 90*, no. 3 (Summer 2005): 299–323.

Forman, Murray. "'Represent': Race, Space and Place in Rap Music." *Popular Music 19*, no. 1 (January 2000): 65–90.

Marchiafava, Louis J., and Charles Stephenson. "A Feeling for Jazz: An Interview with Arnett Cobb." *The Houston Review: History and Culture of the Gulf Coast 12*, no. 3 (1990): 123–43.

Painter, Nell Irvin. "Bias and Synthesis in History." *The Journal of American History 74*, no. 1 (June 1987): 109–12.

Salaam, Mtume ya. "The Aesthetics of Rap." *African American Review 29*, no. 2 (Summer 1995): 303–15.

Scase, Richard. "Review of the Coming of Post-Industrial Society: A Venture in Social Forecasting by Daniel Bell." *The British Journal of Sociology 25*, no. 4 (December 1994).

Steward, James B. "Message in the Music: Political Commentary in Black Popular Music from Rhythm and Blues to Early Hip-Hop." *Journal of African American History 90*, no. 3 (Summer 2005): 196–225.

Electronic Sources

"H.E.R.E. Project Legacy Awards—Celebrating 25 Years of Hip-Hop in Houston." March 23, 2010. Houston Enriches Rice Education - H.E.R.E. Project. file. http://edtech.rice.edu/www/?option=com_iwebcast&task=webcast&action=details&event=2185.

"Jay-Z in Conversation with Cornel West and Paul Holdengräber." November 15, 2010. Fora.TV. http://fora.tv/2010/11/15/Decoded_Jay-Z_in_Conversation_with_Cornel_West.

"A Screwed Up History: Welcome." March 28, 2012. Awready!: Houston Hip Hop Conference. http://lws.lib.uh.edu/hiphop/djscrew/index.html.

INDEX

INDEX

S

ABOUT THE AUTHOR

Maco L. Faniel, a native Houstonian, is an emerging scholar, writer, speaker and advocate. At the time of publication, Maco was a first-year doctoral student in history at Rutgers University. He holds an MA in history from Texas Southern University and a BA in speech and communications from Texas A&M University. He is interested in the social and cultural history of the twentieth-century United States, with particular focus on the ways in which marginalized groups made meaning of American life.

For more info, visit www.macofaniel.com.

Courtesy of Mark Francis, M. Francis Creative.

Visit us at
www.historypress.net
....
This title is also available as an e-book